From Madness to
Jesus

Byron Alexander

Copyright © 2023 Byron Alexander

All rights reserved. No part of this publication may be reproduced, distributed, or transmitted in any form or by any means, including photocopying, recording, or other electronic or mechanical methods, without the prior written permission of the author, except in the case of brief quotations embodied in critical reviews and certain other noncommercial uses permitted by copyright law.

Title: From Madness to Jesus
Author: John Alexander

ISBN: 978-0-9912341-3-4

Publisher: Self-publishing services by Special Novels

website: *specialnovels.com*

Printed in USA
First Edition: 2023

For permission requests, write to the author at the following address: johnny.spotty@gmail.com

All rights reserved.

To order the book or ebook, visit Amazon.com and search for "**From Madness to Jesus**" by *Byron Alexander*.

INDEX

Preface..1
My Dedication and Acceptance of Jesus..................................9
A Thought from Detox...12
Short Memories of Early Thoughts...14
Jealousy unto Others..32
God, Can We Talk?..33
God's Miracles...34
1st, 2nd, or 3rd Class?..35
The Few...37
The Peacemakers..38
I'm Here..39
Hush the Raging Child..40
Children Know Not...42
A Child's Thoughts..43
Baby Steps...46
Children Do Their Dance..47
Innocence Reborn..48
In Search of My Father..50
Don't Give Up, Just Listen...51
Children Please Stay..52
God Commands..53
God's Little Baby...54

A Mother's Hope...55

Try My Shoes..56

A Child's Love..59

Cool Kids...61

A Child's True Nightmare (Part I)....................................63

Have We Ever Met?..106

Life...107

They Touch Me...108

Going Home..109

Through My Eyes...110

The Shadow of the Cross...111

A Different Light..112

Friendship is Genuine..113

They Shine like Their Shoes..114

When the Light Comes On..115

God is the Cure...116

My Strength is God's Guidance....................................118

I Fear Only One..119

Humility: To Be or Not to Be..120

Stepping Away From the Saddle...................................122

The Lone Spirit...124

Saving Ammunition...125

God Teach Me How to Pray..127

Back from the Past...129

You've Touch Me..130
Filling My Heart..131
We..133
Just a Wooden Wheel...134
The Stamp..135
Father I Need a Hug..136
Love Thy Neighbor..137
Divine Serenity...138
Poetry..139
Inner Peace..140
A Child's True Nightmare (Part II)...........................141
Lost Inside Me..169
He is Coming Soon...170
Open Says He..171
No More!..172
There is Little Time, for I Am Time.........................173
His Glorious Task..174
A Witness to You...175
For My Son..176
One of a Kind Blood...177
Knowing Yourself Through God...............................179
My Delight for God's Words......................................181
Is There Jesus in Your Heart?.....................................182
Who's Running the Show?..184

Turn it Over	185
God's Perfect Pitch	186
Let Me Expound Your Name	187
The Power of Praise	188
Ask and Ye Shall Receive	189
Sin or Score	190
The Running Man	191
No Love Lost with Jesus	192
God's Will	193
Pictures We Paint	194
A Façade to God	195
A Walk in Time	197
Awesome Power in Jesus	199
The Other Side	200
I will be Gentle with Myself	201
Clean you Heart and the Mind will Follow	203
God's Love and Grace	205
Satan Roars, So You Won't Deplore	206
Two Paths	207
When Someone Has Fallen	208
The Battle Between God and Evil	209
Oppression	210
Evils Wear a Smile	211
Are You Clean?	212

Man and Nature	215
Nature's Threat, Ready or Not	218
No Future Without Hope	219
Nature's Way	221
Mammals: Our Friends?	222
Face Your Fears	223
Can We Trust	224
A Tree, or a Big Stick with Leaves?	225
Making Amends	226
They Point the Finger	227
Stand for Fight	228
Guide Me	229
Remove These Chains	230
Pray, Obey, Be Amazed	231
Waiting for God's Choice	232
What We Gain with Praise	233
So What Now?	234
Receiving the Seed	236
God's Talk	237
Riding the Line	238
Great Expectations	239
Games People Play	241
Learning	243
Violence or Blindness	244

I Am but a Stone	246
Over and Over	247
Silence is Golden	248
I Can Feel Love Now	249
First Gift of Christmas	250
Think Before You Speak	252
Too Tough	254
No Love in the Bottle, Just the Walking Dead	256
My Earthy Guide	259
A White Dead End	261
Something They Said	263
Relapse	265
Friends	267
Acceptance	268
A New Path	269
It's Just Growth	270
I May Be Poor, but I Am Rich	271
Christmas Wish	273
Do Not Complain	274
The Rose	276
One of One	277
No Regrets	279
God's Strength	280
777	281

Times Heal All..282

Chasing the Breeze...283

Growing...285

Pain..286

Truth..287

I Can't Explain..288

Irritable Twinge..289

Low Hanging Board...290

The Eternal Quest for Christ...291

Know Your Enemy...292

I Am My Final Authority...296

Why We Run in Fear?..299

"Man takes a drink, the drink takes a drink, then the drink takes the man"

~Edward Rolland

PREFACE

There came a time in 1995 I had almost convinced myself that my life was destined to fail. Just two months prior to that, I checked myself into the Veterans Mental Hospital because I was ready to kill myself in sobriety. My PTSD was tearing my life apart. You would think being clean for well over one year that the nightmares would cease, but the thoughts echoed through my head, creating ghostly images that now haunted me during the day. I just couldn't shake them. All I was looking for was someone to hear my cries for help. But because of my background files from treatment, many were saying I was fabricating my stories just to get attention. I've looked back into my files and have read what they have written about me. They all have different dates, times, and places, even the wrong people who actually did the abuse. I could go on and on, but God and I really know what happened, and here is a brief testimony of what darkened any dreams I may have had.

My violent thoughts tormented me tremendously for thirty-eight years to the point of driving me back and forth from the bar to the curb for a total of twelve years. From the age of sixteen, I was considered by most to be a stone-cold alcoholic and drug addict. I had many talents; but I was told I was a loser, didn't try hard enough, and I would never amount to anything, this riddled through my already insecure young mind that drove me to cover my pain any way that I could. I had no idea who I was or what purpose I was supposed to serve in this messed-up maze.

Feeling I had run out of options, I allowed somebody to convince me that I needed treatment. Well, that lasted about two weeks and they kicked me out because they said I wasn't serious about my program. They were right. To me, the world was a joke, and so was my life. Thinking they were all idiots and I'll show you who's not serious.

I continued on and on, trudging through life from job to job, from house to house, until people were tired of helping me slowly kill myself with drugs and alcohol. My second time through treatment, I found out why I couldn't stand to be touched by another man or why I couldn't have any long-lasting relationships with any women. I felt humiliated knowing that I had blocked this all out. Seeing the perpetrator and feeling the emotions made me feel sick and helpless, now that I knew where my nightmares were coming from.

All these problems linked together made me realize that John wasn't all there. These frightening events that had taken place were just the tip of the iceberg. Being taken away not once but twice to Foster homes is why I have the fear of being abandoned. The first time is what traumatized me the most, with unexplainable nightmares and endless sweats. It brought on countless thoughts of suicide and many attempts by loading the rig with the best cocaine, an amount that would kill most people; only to come to with the needle still in my arm, missing the rush and still alive! I have never admitted this to anyone; until now.

The reason I'm still alive is because I know God was there all those times protecting me for this very purpose of sharing my testimony with others. The reason I never told anybody about my suicidal tendencies and attempts,was the fear of being locked away somewhere, never to return to society again. I think one of the reasons I thought this way is because of my father's advice he gave me when he left us. He told me, "Son, you're the oldest and now the man of the house, so here is some advice. "Stand tall, don't cry, and don't ever show any signs of being weak; you have to remain strong for your mother." I was five years old at the time.

You're all thinking, how does he remember all this? The funny thing is I mostly remember the bad things, except for being born, that was a good thing. So you see, everything that happened in my life had an impact on the entirety of my existence. My mother thought I was crazy when I told her that I remember being born, also being in the womb, but that's another story. The point I'm trying to make is that my life was a mess and going nowhere slowly. It was a constant digging into a shallow grave.

All together, I have been in treatment four times. Once was very extensive, aggression therapy lasting for seven months, and then out-patient for another five. I just couldn't get what they were trying to tell me. I was so frustrated, and by this time, so were they. Well, my sobriety lasted a year and a half until I relapsed in Eugene, Oregon. I had really lost it; it was time to check out! All that I had achieved was lost in one night, I couldn't deal with the shame and embarrassment. But once again, God intervened and subconsciously led me to the right people that would help me, which I'll explain in this book along with God's poetic gift he bestowed upon me.

They directed me towards White City Veterans Hospital, which was located in Medford, Oregon. Under strict guidelines, for two months, because of my past three treatments. I drank again, pulling the rug out from under myself, and once again nowhere to go. So I packed up my things with what little money I had made while working in the hospital woodshop and headed towards Portland, Oregon, hoping to get some sympathy from my mother. Well, I got sympathy, but not from my mother. It was New Year's Eve, soon to be 1996. I got to Portland pretty well lit but still functional. I had no brakes, except for the parking brake; and by the way, I had been driving like this for nine hours, and uncountable miles and days prior to this.

It hadn't rained for some time, and the roads were slick. Suddenly, the light changed too fast for me to stop, so I punched it trying to make the next light before it changed. No such luck. I saw the front of my car just miss broadsiding the first car as I entered the intersection at about thirty-five miles per hour. Then "wham," I got hit in the rear. Thank God the guy hesitated when the light changed, or else I would have killed the person that was driving. I ended up sliding over into oncoming traffic and managed to steer back to my side of the road and knocked over a no parking sign coming to a halt. I checked for injuries in the other car and everyone was alright. I didn't want to get the Police involved because I had been drinking, but they weren't going for that.

Just before the Police had arrived, a guy walked up to me and handed me a cup of coffee and I refused, then I changed my mind knowing the coffee would mask the smell of the alcohol. Then I looked up in the sky and very seriously prayed to God. I said, "God, I can't handle going to jail or the financial responsibility of a DUI; and if you don't help me right now, I'll never come back to you ever again." Well, God did one of his miracles. When the Police showed up, the officer looked in the front seat of the car and could see the bottle of MD 20/20 and several quarts of beer. When the officer was finished, without saying a word, he handed me a ticket for an expired license and no insurance. I asked him if he was going to cite me for knocking over the no parking sign and he just shook his head no in response. You know; even the people who were involved in the accident didn't say a word. As they were towing away my car, I told the people who I had hit that I would take care of the damage as soon as I could and they agreed. I looked up in the sky, thanking God for his gracious mercy. So you see; I don't care if you were the Mayor's Son, anyone would have gone to jail in that situation. From that point on,

God was pulling the strings.

I made my way over to Vancouver, Washington, to Hooper Detox looking for a place to sleep and something to eat, at least for a few days. Also, it would better my chances of getting into the CARRS treatment program once again, which was just three blocks away. Well, they didn't have any bed openings until the next day. So when I left there, I was so hungover and tired, all I wanted to do was go to sleep. But God was very loud and was telling me to go to the Veterans Hospital and register for an open bed in treatment. Guess what? Somebody didn't show up for their appointment and took me right in. Long story short, after six days in Detox, I was accepted into treatment for the fourth time.

After I had finished treatment, I went to Detox looking for some direction. They told me of two places. One was called Share House where you could stay for three days at a time; the other was a Men's Ministry, they said I probably wouldn't want to go there. But little did they know that's right where I was supposed to be. I went through the interview and was accepted in. I thought everything was going great; I knew I was right where I belonged. But there were a couple of people there that I found out later were working and doing drugs on the weekends when the elders weren't around. They felt compelled to try and convince the elders and the others that I was playing games and should be thrown out; I had only been there one week.

As I listened from upstairs, Satan began filling my mind with fear and doubt, and I was ready to run once more. I was still so messed up inside, and hearing what they were saying, I couldn't see my life changing, for I wasn't any good; so I was told. When I started packing, I was so angry and hurt, I started crying out loud and asking God why he was allowing this to happen to me! My heart was suddenly broken as I dropped my pride, crying out to God with my face in my pillow, letting out a gut-wrenching scream followed by streaming tears and mucus flowing from my nose. I called out his name and begged for his help. I told him I couldn't run anymore. Unexpectedly, I felt a warm feeling that I recognized from when I was three and a half years old, beaten near to death and dying in a locked closet.

Then there was the most heartfelt thing that God could have ever said to me. He whispered in my ear and said, "I've been with you all this time, all you had to do was ask, I've been waiting for so long for you to meet my Son, and I've also removed your foul mouth in Jesus' name." This is when I felt Jesus enter my heart, and I accepted the Holy Spirit. Well, I cried and cried as God slowly soothed my lost and weary soul.

Besides having Jesus in my heart and removing my foul mouth, letting him share his voice with me was one of God's greatest gifts he could have ever given me.

The next day, I didn't even realize that I hadn't sworn all day, which was brought to my attention by another member. In the past, I tried to quit swearing, as many could attest to the severity of my language. I mean how else could I profess God's truth with the (F) word entangled in my speech? Well, about six months later, God came to me and told me he wanted me to write poetry about him and the darkness I went through. The funny thing is, I kind of felt like Moses when I said, "God, I can't write poetry!" He said, "I'll give you the words." Unlike Moses, I trusted him for the words and he didn't fail me. What God puts in my mind and flows through my heart could have never been accomplished except through God, Amen? He gave me a vision of his book being published, and through a prophet, he said it would be a success. Also, I needed to be patient and he would put the right people in my life for his book to be published, and this book is called "FROM MADNESS TO JESUS."

I dedicate these poems to our Lord God and Jesus Christ, as well as to the struggling people of the world who are earnestly searching for a better way of living. May these words bring comfort, inspiration, and a renewed sense of hope to all.

MY DEDICATION AND ACCEPTANCE OF JESUS

This book contains poems that show different variations of how God and His Son Jesus saved and changed my life. Once I accepted I had no control, and I couldn't manage my own life, things began to change. It took me many, many years to figure out that it just wasn't believing in God; you had to have His Son as the Mediator to the father. That's why so many people say that they believe in God but not His Son, and they wonder why God doesn't answer their prayers. It's really hard to explain to others and describe what happened unless you've experienced it yourself.

There is one thing I would suggest: when you're early in recovery from anything, don't try to do it all at once. When I thought I had everything all figured out and doing the things in my recovery I was supposed to, I began to spin. I thought to myself, "What's going on here Lord? I'm doing what you expect of me, why no change?" Well, there was no answer. So I went to my knees and began to pray like I've never prayed before. I totally got honest with God and surrendered my pride, my sins, criticizing, judging, intellectualizing, and of course, the biggy, blaming others for my problems and defeats.

I began to feel weak and helpless as I prayed for God's forgiveness. I cried out to God and said, "Help me Lord, I can't do this anymore!" I knew that if I didn't give it all up right here, right now, I was going to end up where I was seven months ago, ready to kill myself in sobriety. There was something missing in my life, and I was about to find out. As I began to let the tears flow from a deep desire to grasp that missing piece of the puzzle that I desperately needed. It felt like warm hands reaching inside me and pulling out the basketball out of my stomach, and the cleansing began.

The poems I've written come from everyday life situations. Some come from childhood memories and the darkness I felt when I was on the street. I hope these poems depict a similar picture as they did for me. Being a recovering alcoholic and addict, I have been through many trials, but I still held onto the fact that God was real and I believed in him, and I know he never gave up on me.

I would briefly like to explain what kind of background I come from. I came from an upper middle class family with a stepfather that knew no other way to raise children except the way he was raised, so I don't blame him anymore. I had a very violent childhood stemming from mental, physical, and sexual abuse. I was also put into a foster home twice, once when I was three and again at five and never knowing why. I thought I was to blame for being there. So from the age of three to the age of six my life was already scattered and torn apart. I hadn't really caught on who God was yet but I knew of his name and what he represented. I believed in something I could not see without any reservations, of course, I didn't really have any yet.

My psychiatrist told me that if I hadn't had my belief in God, I would have and could have killed myself or someone else long before this. So if I could change from a former foul-mouthed, drug-addicted mind and lifestyle into the person I am today. Then others can do the same if they're willing to accept someone they cannot see, then they could open their hearts and their minds. I"m not saying that it will all go away, it depends on your background like me. I ask for forgiveness many times in a day, but hey, that's me. So how can it hurt to try something new compared to how your life is now, or are you just too tough?

From Madness to Jesus

This is something I wrote during my fourth attempt to get clean and sober, specifically when I was going through the detox process. At that time, my overall outlook on life was quite bleak, especially as I observed the people who seemed consumed by negativity and destructive behaviors in our world.

A Thought from Detox

The means to an end are the beginning of death. Can we see past this and resist temptation? Not if we can't find what's ailing us, depriving us the right to live. There are many who aren't able to fix themselves. Some think it's a safe move to use a scalpel rather than love and support. Staying sober seems to be my ultimate goal, but misery gets in my way, tempting fate once more. Each time I bounce back, I learn a little more, and I become determined as my natural talents emerge. This I could have never hoped for in the past. Reality is too frightening for me to comprehend. I am afraid of everyone and everything because none of it seems real to me. That's why I remain hard and untested. I remain a secret to everyone concerned, allowing my defenses to ensure my strength. My fear of being weak is my demise. A foreign particle which has infected my soul and continues to grow, affecting my spiritual well-being. When I see others around me, it angers my soul to see people hurting each other, and it starts a churning inside me that wants to step on every cockroach I see that can't conceive life the way it's supposed to be.

Unless I can stop looking at world pain and hunger as an unthinkable threat, I won't be able to stop the pain I feel inside me. This child has seen it, felt it, and experienced this warped sense of love and will not allow anyone to do this ever again. I love animals, children, I love elderly people, and God's awesome florals because I can learn something from each one of them. But I can't stand unbalanced people who feel inflicting pain on others is their source of love. Until this becomes an accepted part of my life, I will continue to relapse because I'm able to escape into a false world which has no reality, no beginning, no abrupt ending, just a slow digging into a shallow grave.

God knows I try, but if I'm not trying hard enough, someone

needs to lead me to the right means of acceptance. My conception outweighs all reasons beyond human factions. This is a truth to a beginning. A reality that waves to me from a faraway place that reminds me of the land of Oz, searching for the wizard to give me a new heart, so I can feel love and compassion for those who don't care for other people's feelings and to truly enjoy what life has to offer. The wheel of life, the circle that never stops on the right number. A continuous spinning cycle that keeps driving me away from the people who really care.

    I don't want to die alone, I don't want to be one of those that life forgot, a stone left unturned that has so much to offer. I'm slowly learning and I'm impatient. I would like all the information at once, but I know what would happen. I would just like to get on with my life with no regrets and help others who are less fortunate than I am. I still can't trust, even though I know I have to one day. Maybe it will happen if I take that giant leap of faith and trust God to run my life.

SHORT MEMORIES OF EARLY THOUGHTS

To begin with, these true stories and God's poems are for those who think life has treated them unfairly. Through my testimony and poems, I will try to show you that everybody gets a different deal, and we're not all the same.

Let me explain. Life is not a bed of roses; it's not about peaches and cream, and it's not a bad dream. It's all about lessons and trials that we all have to face. You know, I look back on how my life was and how it seemed similar to the way Jesus started out. I'm not saying I suffered like Jesus; what I'm saying is this. I was treated as an outcast at an early age, from as far back as I can remember, even at Church during recess, after Bible studies. I didn't go through what Jesus did, but later on, my life was much more violent than his; just because I was different.

I recall all the times growing up when I mentioned God or Jesus. I was either picked on, laughed at, or beat up. I look back on the story and birth of Jesus, how the Angels helped Joseph and Mary to guide them to another town whenever Jesus was in danger. This was so the prophecy could be fulfilled. Now, in my case, this was different. My parents had to go on their own instincts of what their parents had taught them. It's called passing on the traditional seed; in every family, this occurs. It's a vicious cycle and it has to stop.

This can only be accomplished if we, and of course, our parents, are willing to take someone else's point of view and weigh them against their own lives. Now it's not easy; no one likes to admit that they've made a mistake when it comes to their children. I know what it's like when someone tells you that you're wrong.

When they try to explain, it's like they're speaking in a different language. Well, basically they are. Until we are able to accept the truth, there will be no change. Let me give you an example. If you have a boy that has been raised deep in the woods, far away from any type of civilization, and let's say he had only his father to teach him all about life. Now one day, his father teaches him that a tree is nothing but a big stick with leaves.

As he grew older, he heard stories from his Dad's friends that had been to the big city, and he decided to find out for himself what it's really like. Packing what he could carry, his father gives him some last-minute advice and sends him on his way. When he gets to the big city, he meets someone, and they soon become friends, and they decide to share a place together. After some time, they were out walking, enjoying a lovely summer's day, and the one from the city looked up and said, "that sure is a big beautiful tree." The boy from the woods laughs and he says, "that's not a tree, that's a big stick with leaves."

Now, what do you think would happen next? Would they each stand their ground for what they had been told? Of course they would. One knew the real truth, but the other was unwilling to listen; because the one person he idolized the most, taught him everything he knew and there's no way his Dad could be wrong. That's why there's so much prejudice in the world today. So many are teaching what they have been taught and are unwilling to change their ways. The truth hits us in the 'ole ego, that word so many are afraid to let go of, because someone may see them as being weak and inept. So what, who cares! Is it really that hard, or are you just too tough? I was taught at an early age that violence was all about being a real "man," taking it and receiving it; "Bzzzzzz," wrong answer!

Violence is not the solution; it only leads to more violence. There's nothing wrong with righteous anger when someone has done you wrong, but it's how far you go with that anger and how we act upon it. Now I'm going to begin by telling you what was the hardest part of my life; and that is, I remember all the way back to being born. I know this is hard to swallow, but it's true.

In recent years, studies have shown that I am not alone. It was such a relief. You see, up until about ten years ago, I thought I was going crazy with these flashes that were constantly going through my mind. I remember everything in detail: the thoughts, emotions, pain, and the nightmares. I had nightmares growing up, as most children do; the problem was mine consisted of not only normal scary dreams but also my haunting past. I still have them every now and then and I am forty five years old. They are not as frequent since I accepted Jesus into my life, but this I know; God does not push the erase button. This stems from my P.T.S.D., post-traumatic stress disorder.

At one time I thought only combat Veterans had it, "Bzzzzzz", wrong answer again. It's brought on by stress, and at times I have plenty of that. Now some are fortunate enough that they don't have this kind of recall and they don't have to re-live their childhood over and over, especially the violent ones; but millions of us do. I would like you all to know that while I'm telling you my story I'm re-living the sick pain and feelings about everything. From three to age sixteen, my life stemmed from violent mental, physical and sexual abuse. Now I'm not sniveling, I'm stating a fact. If you take a young child, chain them, beat them senseless telling them how worthless they are for countless years, that's all they'll know. Eventually they will turn into a wild dog pissing on any tree they can. Oh sure, they will have intermittent spurts of sensitivity that's in all of us; but kick the dog and see what happens. Here is the chain of events that happened and created the world in which I lived.

When I was two years old and I believe we lived in Corpus Christi Texas, my father used to give me beer before putting me down for a nap. I remember standing in front of the refrigerator and my father would grab a beer and pour it into my bottle. I would lie down in my crib and remember the warm fuzzy feeling I would get from the brown bottle; my mother found out he was doing this and she told him that there would be no more of that. So my father tried substituting apple juice for the beer but that didn't work. I would go lye down for my nap and I knew there was something odd; I wasn't getting the desired effect I had before and it tasted

different. I would scream until my father would come back into my room and I would hold the bottle out to him and he knew what I wanted. He tried fooling me a couple of times, but I watched as he would grab the bottle of beer and the apple juice at the same time trying to make me think there was beer in my bottle; I would throw a fit and always win. This was not the first time I had alcohol. My mother told me many years ago that my father would put vodka in my bottle when I was a baby to make me stop crying. So you see, the mind never forgets no matter how old you are.

From Corpus Christi Texas and until I was three, I don't recall my Dad being around. I believe this is when he joined the navy. We then moved to Kodiak Island in Alaska. We lived in a small trailer amongst many others. At this time I'm about two and a half and hell on two legs. I would like to share a quick story about my guardian Angel. Now if you are a true believer in Christ then you'll know what I'm about to tell you is the truth and can only be described as a spiritual happening. I was a child that needed to be watched at all times. One day my mother had to go to the Navel store which was off the Island and she would be gone most of the day, so the neighbor was watching me but she had fallen asleep. Near the trailer park was a small quarry that had no fences surrounding it. I remember walking for a ways with the breeze blowing slightly as it always does and I noticed the ground began to slope downward. As I got closer I saw the ground disappear. This made me hesitant as I slowed my step and inched my way forward one foot at a time.

I remember seeing the edge and I started to lean forward. For a split second I saw huge boulders a long way down and suddenly out of the corner of my eye I s.aw the ground break behind me and I started to fall as my hands went into the air; at that moment I felt a hand grab me by the back of my shirt and pulled me on the other side of the break and sat me down on the dirt. I quickly turned around to see who had saved me and there was o one there. I remember standing and seeing where the ledge had given way and I knew that it did happen. Staying far from the edge, I walked a ways and I saw a road leading down towards the pit. I walked down the road and over to the boulders I had seen just before I started to fall.

As I got closer, I saw all the dirt that had come from above. Now at my age, 30 feet would be a long way, but this was near fifty feet. I was only about two and a half but I knew that if I had fell that far on all those rocks, I would have died. This would not be the last time I would be saved by the grace of God. When I returned to the trailer the lady who was watching me was frantic when I walked back in, and by the way you're probably wondering how I just walked in and out of the trailer. It was very small, the kind one person would get claustrophobic in. Needless to say she was very grateful yet hysterical when she saw me and also very enthusiastic to make me some hot chocolate.

After a short time there we moved to Bremerton Washington where I had been born. This was where most of my relatives lived and where the nightmare began. We lived in Navel housing and to this day it's still there and unchanged by time. I'm three by now and really becoming a handful. I had a bad habit of wandering, as most of the kids my age didn't interest me much. I tried playing with the older kids but they were always giving me a bad time about not having a father. I told them that I did but they didn't believe me. I was what they called the bastard child. I continually had to defend myself saying, "I do have a father and you can ask my mother!"

One day my mom was outside and I dared them to ask if I had a father. Well they couldn't pass up a dare so they asked her. She told them yes he does have a father and he will be coming home soon. This would have been true if my father wasn't constantly being thrown in the brig for some kind of beef. Every time I would get my hopes up that he was coming home, I would be disappointed once again and the other kids were convinced that it was all a lie. Now labeled as a liar, they began treating worse than before.

They isolated me from joining in on their social activities. I soon felt like an outcast from the whole neighborhood. I began amusing myself by making up fictitious friends to play with. To make matters worse, my mother noticed I wasn't playing with the other kids any more and asked me why. I told her they were always beating on me because they thought I lied about my father. She decided to have a talk with them. When she returned she told me everything had been straightened out and to go next door and play. Well I don't need to tell you what happened next. I got mouthy telling them I told you so and this didn't sit well with them at all. Because of my mother intervening and my mouth, they ran me off, with sticks and rocks.

I came home crying and my mother let me stay inside for the rest of the day. Early next morning the doorbell rang and my mom answered the door. It was one of the neighbor kids wanting to know if I could come outside and play. I told my mom they didn't want to play, they just wanted to beat me up again. My mom said, "no they don't, now go outside and play." It wasn't fifteen minutes before I came running back in the house with a black eye. My mother had enough! She went and talked with a couple of mothers and expressed her concerns and her anger, mainly because of the age difference. Needless to say my mother apologized for doubting me and she was very sorry. She let me stay inside for a couple of days during the afternoon; as I would play outside early in the morning before the other kids got out of bed. My good little boy attitude didn't last long, as I had a little brother and I was beginning to take out my aggressions on him. I began breaking things; and when my mother would come to see what happened I would blame it on my brother. I got away with it for quite some time as my brother, "by the way his name is Mike", wasn't really old enough to speak up for himself, or comprehend what actually was going on, because he was barely two years old at the time.

My mother began to think it was odd that my brother had never broken this many things even when he was younger learning how to walk and new things were within his reach. My mother was keeping a close eye on us while we were playing, and one day she caught me breaking an ashtray and I was sent.to my room for the day. The following day she decided it was time for me to go outside and play. She thought since I didn't have friends to play with that she allowed me to take my brother outside with me. I can remember the wicked thoughts that went through my mind at the time. I could torment him and get away with it because he would be out of her sight. As I mentioned he was barely two and still a little uncoordinated, it was really easy to knock him off balance. I can't believe I got pleasure seeing him cry, but at that time I did. My mother would come outside and see what happened and I would say,"oh mommy he's so clumsy." She believed me the first few times, but after three days in a row she laid in wait for me. She would watch from the bedroom window. I would take him around the side of the house out of her sight; so I thought.

One day she caught me pushing him down and she came running outside and took my brother in the house saying I didn't deserve to play with him. Well she was right. I had so much hate towards the other kids that I didn't even have love for my brother. It was lonely with no friends. This is where I really started to change. I was so negative, I spent all my energy trying to invent new ways to antagonize and get my brother in trouble. I could come up with a long list of all the things I did, but it would make me out to be some kind of child monster. The bottom line; I was torturing Mike beyond comprehension: I went as far one day by biting my brother from head to foot, not breaking the skin, but leaving bruises all over his body.

This social isolation was beginning to bring out an aggressive illness. I was unaware obviously of my escalating problem and neither was anybody else. One day we were left with a babysitter and while she was in the other room, I offered my brother a whole bottle of children's aspirin because it tasted like candy. I had no idea of the outcome of this awful mistake. The babysitter soon had to call my mother, as there was something terribly wrong with Mike. When she came home my brother was crying uncontrollably. His crying was so severe she decided to take him to the hospital. At the hospital, doctors didn't know what the problem was so they sent him home. I remember sitting in the back seat and my mother holding Mike and he was screaming at the top of his lungs. When we got home, my mother asked the babysitter to get the children's aspirin thinking that might help. She couldn't find them.

My mother wanted Mike's baby blanket also, so the babysitter went to get it. Lifting the blanket up, the empty bottle of aspirin dropped on the floor and she showed it to my mother. Seeing that he had consumed the whole bottle, she went back to the hospital. On the way there she was trying to figure out how he got a hold of them. She asked the babysitter if she had given him any and if she had left them in the crib by accident. She replied she hadn't.

When we arrived, she told the doctors about the aspirin and now they knew how to treat him. They couldn't pump his stomach because it had already worked its way into his system; all they could do was give him something to stabilize his situation. My mother came out of the room and asked me if I had given the aspirin to him and I told her I did, but I didn't know it would make him cry like that. The doctors explained to her, if they hadn't known about the aspirin he would have died; basically burning from the inside out. Now, can you understand why from now on my mother wasn't going to trust me to be alone with my brother?

Even though I was genuinely sorry for what I had done, I didn't really grasp the seriousness of the situation. After that event, I was much more affectionate towards my brother, but my mother still didn't trust me. I had to earn her trust all over again. Now I'd like to step away for just a moment and say that this part of my life had some positive impact later growing up. The positive is for the women and children that have been in my life; because they didn't have to suffer at the hands of my self destructive rage. This I had promised to God; and as far as I know this is probably the only promise that I had truly ever kept.

Oh sure in my mind the theater still played their roles, but I played them to the end and weighed the outcome of what it would do to my soul. Now as you remember my mother kept telling me that my father was coming home, but I was continually being disappointed. With all the pessimistic attitudes coming from the other kids in the neighborhood I was beginning to think that maybe they were right and my mother was lying to me.

But one day I was playing outside, a taxi pulled up and this man stepped out and stood towering over me; and I said, "Are you my daddy?" He looked down at me and said, "Where is your mother?" I pointed back at the house as he walked right by me. I stood there not knowing what to think. Then suddenly I felt sick as he walked outside holding my brother in his arms and giving me a dirty look. My father was angry at me and I didn't even know why. I hadn't seen him since I was two and all the defending I did for him with the other kids went right out the window, along with my guts spilt all over the sidewalk. He said something to the effect that I was a bad boy and that I should be ashamed of myself for what I had done. That was two weeks ago and I had already been at the whipping post and as far as I knew I had been forgiven.

Here I was three years old and my father was putting me back in the gutter from which I was trying to return. I was devastated by his hatred towards me. I started to cry as I ran to the side of the house and felt worthless and isolated from the whole family and the father I had waited for all this time now didn't want anything to do with me. The window was open and I heard my father say he was taking Mike to the store with him and I watched from the corner of the house as he walked away. This broke my heart as I started to choke on my tears and I felt like running away. You say, run away? You all have to understand, I may have only been three, but I was walking at nine and a half months and talking at one and a half years old. On several occasions I would wander off a half mile or so towards the main drag of town and my mother would find me later. After several times the guys at the gas station would call my mother and say, "He's wondering again, do you want to come and get him.

Anyway, while my father was gone I came in the-house crying and told her how upset I was and she said she would talk to him. When my father had returned she told him what I had said and he called me inside the house and sat me on his lap and explained to me what I had done was wrong. I listened to his every word, because he was my father. My mother stood there as he talked to me and then she suggested that he take me to the store too. Well I felt secure when he agreed and held me in his arms. We left the house, with me on his shoulders strolling down the road on a memorable journey.

That is the last thing I remember at that point about my father as far as actually seeing him.

You know what really hurts me right now? In 1995 on my 39th Birthday, my brother brought up the incident about the aspirin event, and accused me that I knew full well what I was doing at the age of three years old. Now l have to say that was one of the most asinine statements I've ever heard him say. You might as well have wrapped a noose around my neck and said that I was a serial killer for all that matter. The worst part about that situation; my mother was backing him up and adding more fuel to the fire. She was doing what my grandmother did to her and my uncles. It was like throwing a piece of meat between two starving dogs.

Years down the road I confronted her on it, and she denies ever saying that. Now my life has been based on remembering all significant negative aspects of my life, and to learn how not to make the same mistakes ever again. Now I did make mistakes over again, just not the bad ones.

For some reason at this point in my life, I decided that it was time to cut myself loose from my family that was tearing my life apart. I really resented them for the way they were treating me and I did not deserve it. I began to see the true meaning of my existence, but l still couldn't stop the thoughts bent on self-destruction. I have been paying for that incident, internally and externally through the guilt and the shame coming from my mother and fathers expectations of how my life should be.

My father to this day has never told me that he loves me. This pain ran so deep I finally had to write to him and tell him I couldn't live like that anymore and that he was going to have to live the rest of his life without me in it. This wasn't easy to do by any means, but it had to be done, for my own peace of mind. Well after I wrote him the letter, I never heard from him again. Of course he never was one for writing.

You see, he has four sons and one daughter. My sister was born after I was taken away which is a little later in my story, and her name is Jackie. She is the only one who helps me and understands the guilt of my past which I carry around my neck. You know what the funny thing is about my father? I think the reason my father hates me is that I must be a constant reminder of his earlier failures, because he did right by my two half brothers. I do know this; that when he dies it will tear my heart out, because despite his expectations of how my life should have gone, I was still a disappointment in his eyes. I still really do love my father; because he is my father. No matter what I do in life, I will always pay for not being a success; and I truly am sorry for not obtaining that goal. I can only say that no matter what happens, my true happiness is my only concern; and that can only be accomplished through God and his Son. You know, to this very day my mother will not tell me the truth of who actually took me to the shelter home and that she said she would never read this book. Well I'm no rocket scientist but I feel it was my Fathe-r because he was still there when I went to bed for the first night without crying myself to sleep. When I woke the next morning I was on the floor of a strange place and not in my own bed. I was paralyzed with fear and my mind out of control; because I was out of my element. I wish I could say that they found me a nice home, but that was a horrifying melancholy.

For this next story will tell you of the sick and perverted reality that I would not wish on my worst enemy. This story is for those who think life has ended for them and there's no use living because God doesn't love you. I'm still alive to this day and only through the grace of God have I survived and lived life on life's terms.

I would like to say to anyone who struggles with pain and guilt from the loss of a parent's love. Don't wait until it's too late like I did to reconcile, because my father died and he didn't get to see me get my life together and for that I truly am sorry. l couldn't even go to his funeral and my stepmother and two half brothers won't talk to me anymore, and I will not carry their shame!

John 93'
   Getting in touch with your inner child... and this is mine!

What is your name?
„MY NAME IS JOHNNY."

How old are you?
„I AM 5 YEARS OLD."

How do you feel?
„I FEEL FINE."

Do you want to tell me about yourself?
„NO, I AM TRAPPED INSIDE YOU."

Why are you so mad?
„BECAUSE OF THE WAY I'VE BEEN TREATED."

Do you want to change?
„YES, BUT NOT UNTIL I LEARN ABOUT YOU AND ME AND WHAT HAPPENED TO US."

Are you afraid?
„YES."

Of what?
„EVERYTHING."

Are you afraid of adults?
„YES."

Why?
„BECAUSE THEY HURT ME ALL OVER."

Can you trust adults?
„NO."

Why?
„BECAUSE THEY DON'T LISTEN TO ME."

Do you want to be loved?
„YES."

Do you know how to love?
„NO."

Do you think you can learn to love?
„YES, BUT I DON'T KNOW HOW TO."

Can you forgive others for what they've done to you?
„I DON'T KNOW."

If I teach you how to love and forgive, do you want to learn?
„YES, PLEASE SHOW ME. I AM AFRAID OF THAT WOMAN."

Can we be friends and helpful to each other?
„I'M CONFUSED."

I want to help you, I want to let you know it's okay to begin to trust.
„NO, I AM NOT READY TO TRUST YET."

I want to love you, do you believe that?
„I DON'T KNOW."

Can you forgive me for forgetting about your needs and wants, instead of being so insensitive towards my needs?

Why did you feel that way towards me?
„BECAUSE I'M MAD AT YOU AND I DON'T WANT TO PLAY ANYMORE."

Okay, I understand. Bye for now.
„GOODBYE."

And this is what happened when I finally accepted Jesus into my life

JEALOUSY UNTO OTHERS

When I was young and nothing really mattered, life seemed so simple, but then it changed and became all torn and tattered.

As I grew, my teachings were to be a man, stand tall, don't cry, and always keep your back against the wall.

This marked the end of my goodness and my introverted way of life of mixed up beliefs and torments in endless flights.

I wandered and ran from everything good that I saw: the people, my friends, even the churches had flaws.

Jealousy haunted my soul, tearing at my morals, keeping me down from feeling whole.

The hopes and dreams turned into endless screams of confusion and nightly schemes.

Jealousy drove me mad, seeing others happy and having fun. I couldn't see any hope in my life, constantly living on the run.

Suddenly, looking at my life, I thought, "How can I feel and live this way?" I paused, and I knew it was time to say, "Alright God, I give up. Set me free and teach me your ways."

Well, He did as I asked, and He heard what I said, as He laid my old ways to rest in my head.

The more I read his wondrous words and spoke of his glory and grace, the more I changed, the better I felt. Suddenly, my life didn't seem so strange.

I glowed and tingled, I moved and mingled, for my gratitude wasn't enough; I had to tell the world through a rhyme and a jingle.

GOD, CAN WE TALK?

Every day, we should bring our problems to God and seek help to get through the day, while we pray for others who won't listen to what we have to say.

It's a never-ending task as we pray and pray, but do we ever sit back and say, "Hey God, how about you and me, let's sit back and talk today?"

You know, God, it seems like everything is a battle as we mix with others and their views, along with the everyday disasters on the news.

How do we find time to share our true love, when there's so much negative response when we mention the heavens above?

Lord, help me understand and feel their pain as they drown their emotions with an imaginary rain.

I know you see the stress and how it bends people to its will. Why not? It's our number one silent deadly disease, always ready to kill.

It whispers an easy solution and rings in your ear: just take another drink, take another pill as you distance your mind further from God's will.

When the pressures are a bit much, just open your arms and accept the Lord's gracious touch.

There's a short poetic prayer that helps me when people fill my mind with their jeering ways. It's so simple, just a short little phrase.

No matter how you feel, what you say, what you think, or what you do, the Jesus in me still loves you.

God's Miracles

We see miracles all around us, in the streets and on the bus; it doesn't matter where we are or where we go, we find that God's miracles aren't just for show.

God's miracles are for us to see and learn to know he's alive and that he really does care, and for us to stop thinking that life is so unfair.

He lets us know, that he's watching from a place so near, he's so close you can hear him whisper in your ear, "I'm here children, so don't you fear, just read my words, and hold them to your heart so dear.

"Guard them with your life, protect them like you would your family or your wife."

We should never neglect his words of love, so soft and healing from the skies above.

God shows his love so many times in his book of truth, and through others in rhymes.

The truth may seem harsh and sometimes unfair, so why should we continue to doubt God and keep pulling out our hair?

His miracles happen not by chance, he shows us when we open our eyes, then he gives us life enhanced.

Like so many times before, he shows his power when he opens the door.

But if we clog our minds with fits of rage for what we found in our way, or when we can't get what we need and found it wouldn't be today; so trivial, so minor, so caught up in time, just listen to this truth, this truth in rhymes.

Let loose of your grip and fall to your knees, to see God's purpose and let him tend to your needs.

1st, 2nd, or 3rd Class?

In this world of segregated classes, we tend to divide and judge ourselves by money and fashion.

It's there for all to see, and as adults we pass on this dubious creed.

We teach our children, and they learn from our remarks, to show no compassion or care because we judge everyone clearly by the style of the clothes they wear.

This segregation isn't just for homes without God; it's present in all walks of life, whether good or bad. It's senseless and cruel, bitter and sad.

Yes, it is sad that we as mere humans take it upon ourselves to play God, looking down on people because they have less money, lower stature, or no power, while the rich view them with disgust peering down from their tall ivory towers.

You see, money replaces the feelings you get when you lend someone a hand, when you set aside those old thoughts you had, for you're able to see the true picture when someone's down and feeling bad.

You know something? I could ask someone who thinks they have it all to trade places with someone who's been shunned by the world, lying in the gutter and crawling. Do you know what they would say? "I don't have to trade with them or live that way because I've worked for what I have, and I have no pity for such a man, a man who has no class and lives day by day from a smelly old can."

Look at the world Satan has painted for us, where we must keep our judgments to ourselves and look down on others with disgust. You people just don't get it, do you? No, you'd rather ride around in your big fancy cars, looking down on people and observing from afar.

Your life is so bitter and cold that you can't even see how Satan has fitted for a cast of a devilish mold.

You know what's even more depressing that I see? In the churches, many still play this role, judging others by what they wear or what they may do, without judging their own souls, pointing fingers on cue.

This is why so many children steer away from God because their parents are still caught up in fashion and façade!

Children observe and play out what they see, adopting a role for power that shuns others for greed.

I have to say, I was one who was raised that way, but when I reached a certain age, I couldn't live with those old thoughts that said, "stand and be a man." So, I offered them my friendship and extended my hand.

I found realism and heart in the people I met. It wasn't about money, and they had no regrets!

For they saw what money does to the heart at large. It takes and takes and gives you nothing in return because people make it evil, to the point where they have so much to burn.

I'd like to leave you all with this cold, hard fact, that I would like the rich to hear and do this simple act.

Give generously, and half of what you have, watch the change in the world it would bring, the many starving people, the dinner bell would surely ring. There would be smiles in the world that would spread so wide, where they once were starving and shaking as they cried, because their life was so desolate, for their stomachs were empty inside.

Oh, how I would love to see the children when the dinner bell rings, joyfully running to their homes with hope and pride, praising the Lord and to God they would joyfully sing.

THE FEW

The Lord says: "Ingest my words and enjoy my fruit, use my words wisely for rebuttal and refute.

The Lord is angry, and many should fear their demise. They're too big to be strong, too little for their lies.

The coming will be quick; even the deaf will hear the soothing sounds of trumpets, along with the bellowing of bitterness and tears.

So show the Lord your will and might, who can beat the best and who can stand and fight.

Because we are the few who consume His words, we are the few who trust on a hopeless night, and we are the few who will stand in darkness while still serving the light.

THE PEACEMAKERS

Pray for God to rescue the lost hearts of the world and surrender their souls to the spirit of the cross.

They know about His love, but they're unwilling to hear because they see too much pain and not the sound of cheer.

God is everywhere; the angels are like His eyes. They see and feel the hurt of the world and send their message to God in the sky.

"Rise up, people, take a stand, wake up your neighbors, and guide their hands!"

"Fill their hearts with a smile of love, then take their hands and lift them high into the sky above!"

Let them feel the spirit of God with His powerful words and His feelings of love!

His strength will increase as you lead others towards the light, but Satan will be there, confusing God's words, saying, "Are you sure this is day, or could it be night?"

The light will shine with truth in their eyes, the truth of God, which darkness will despise!

Let love fill your heart, and God will fill your eyes, with the true meaning of grace, and hold your hands high in the sky; PRAISE GOD, THIS IS NOT A LIE!

God wants you to live like you're going home, to fear only Him, to what you have been shown.

For fear is nothing but a word, just a thought, a feeling, just something you heard.

So remember, live your life like you're going home; stand with heart, hope, and love; for God will reveal to us what we have learned, and then He'll continue with His Holy Grace, giving you strength and faith, and of course, more challenges to face.

I'm Here

I know He's here when I see the rain, I know He's here when I feel the pain, I know He's here when I reach for the sky, I know He's here when He soothes me when I cry.

There's nothing like feeling God's soft touch, to some, it doesn't seem like much, and to countless many, they fail to see it as such.

But to those who believe, who go to their knees, will feel like a child of God, tugging on His sleeve.

They can always feel safe from any harm if they're just willing to tug on His arm.

HUSH THE RAGING CHILD

From the moment of birth, there was a seed of rage, a feeling of loss, that guided a cage.

A fire that was built with such force, removing all feelings, and it had to run its course.

Hush the raging child's fear, this couldn't be done, for there were no tears.

The rage lived on through day and night, living in terror, with blinding fists of might.

Though a child, he showed no fear, desperately needing to be held dear.

Many discarded his cries of pain, for no one knew this child, this child like Cain.

They passed him from arm to arm, but no one kept him safe from harm.

They shouted, they raged, they threw up their hands, they said, "We can't keep him, there's too much demand!"

They all saw the child as a devil in disguise, but no ears were open to his fearful cries.

They beat him down again and again, all they saw was a raging child saying, "I'll beat you and win!"

All he wanted to convey to all concerned, a love that was lost and he wanted returned.

He knew guilt and shame too well, words that kept coming from the gates of hell.

So he searched in vain, trying desperately to find a love to gain.

He couldn't seem to find the love he had lost, but he held his ground, refusing to give up at any cost.

He reached a point where he had lost all fight, and Satan beat him down, and he lost all sight.

The end was almost near as he stomped his feet and filled his eyes with tears, while Satan said, "I want your soul because you're no good. You tried and tried and didn't do what you should!"

Satan almost won, cluttering his mind with a blood-filled room, but he stood up crying out to God, stomping his feet, while Satan still trying to seal his doom.

He raged and cried like a child, asking God to help him from committing the ultimate sin, asking God for the strength to beat Satan and win.

God interceded, as he always had, telling the raging child, "Be strong, little lad."

Knowing what to do, he ran from the room, fleeing from Satan and his ultimate doom.

He humbled himself as he reached out to a friend, and through God, a message he did send.

With meekness in his heart, and God renewed his mind, God held him in His arms, saying, "I've been with you all this time."

So you see, God shows His mercy to the weak, and scolds those who linger too long in the street. God will always be there to soothe the raging child, defending you from the savage beast and the ultimate trial.

CHILDREN KNOW NOT

Children nowadays have their minds all mixed up in a whirling craze. They feel they're going nowhere, and their lives are caught in a gigantic maze.

I remind you, children, do not complain and think that life is so unfair, because Satan will confuse you even more, making you slowly believe that God doesn't care.

If you have a complaint, before you seek God, here's what to do: remind yourself of the handicapped people of the world, and your mind can quickly snap back, relieving those selfish thoughts and reminding you of where you're at.

Let's try something different; when you're wandering and lost, look around you and set your eyes on the scampering of innocent little tots. See how they dance in their own little world, without any sin or even a selfish thought.

I don't know about you, but when I see them I choke when I laugh, because I feel their souls float on that freedom stream of air, trusting anyone who shows them true love and care.

Their minds are clean and in God's own hands, their eyes darting all around, catching anything they can.

Children can be taught to remain that way if they're shown early the importance of amends and how to pray.

For their sake, show them by our examples and break the chains that bind our souls to earth. Tell them all about God and show them true love and self-worth.

A Child's Thoughts

The inner child is so full of life, so wild with sugar, and yet so full of strife.

Inside, the child has hidden pain, trying to hold dearly onto what he's gained.

His little feet may go pitter-patter, all the time thinking... nothing really matters.

All the while, when he's really hurt, he still trusts once more, giving you anything he can, even his shirt.

He's looking for love from anyone he can, trying to make heads or tails of this strange land.

Striving in life to find new ways, things become dismal again, like being in a haze.

Before, when he was young, his eyes were sparkling and bright, now they've become foggy, as he's confused by the ways of the light.

In his confusion, he feels there's nowhere to turn, he suddenly loses sight, and his old ways return.

Feeling trapped, like a mouse in a maze, searching for an exit and forever gaining ground, without God, this will never be found.

He still can't find what he's looking for, all he needs is to be nurtured, to feel safe once more.

What he's learned, he tries to put into practice, but finds it doesn't work, these inherited tactics.

Finally, he falls to his knees, and God shows him a better way, once again he learns to trust, and decides this time he'll stay. As he grows and gains more knowledge untold, God sends him courage, and things begin to unfold.

The child inside still remembers, but soon learns to forgive, for those who have harmed him, and now he's willing to live.

At last, he's found peace in a hostile land, Jesus has warmed his heart, now the nightmares will forever cease, as God continues to lead him by the hand.

I dedicate this segment to my mother, whom I am grateful for her help when I was down, despite her misgivings.

After I write truthful poems of God's words manifested inside me, it saddens my heart to know that there are people in this world who don't care for God.

Not the ones who believe, but the ones who are into money and greed. I have lived my life hoping to become that person I once was, so innocent at birth, feeling that 100% trust in someone besides myself.

Oh, but to be that weak, frail child, one of God's miracles for whom fear was nothing, not even a word.

I'm thinking back, lying in my mother's arms, her soft soothing voice comforting my blameless mind and telling me, "I'll protect you, son. Shhh, hush little baby, don't cry, be still, Mommy's here, don't cry."

It was such a beautiful feeling being in Mommy's arms, feeling the total surrender under God's watchful eyes. "Oh people, can't you remember what it was like? Have we all forgotten?" I haven't; I still feel the warm, soft blanket that enveloped me in the security of my mother's arms.

If we could grasp that thought, hold it dear to our hearts, and then pass it on to our children's children, "Oh, what an inheritance." A gift from God that no one can take away. We can say, "that's just a dream, the world is too evil!" Well, I say boo to evil; if you have God in your hearts and believe that the sufferings are not of God and you surrender completely, you'll find in time and remember that feeling you once had, wrapped safely in that blanket in your mother's arms. Amen!

BABY STEPS

Putting one foot in front of the other, it seemed so hard when we tried. Our parents cheered us on, giving us hope, and soon they began to cry.

When we became of age and thought we knew it all, our parents cried once again, asking, "What happened? Why didn't they call?"

They taught us their ways and what we needed to know, but they forgot when we called, when we needed them so.

Parents, you need to learn new ways to teach your children how not to stray.

It's words from God that keep us all in step. We need to learn when we're young; your children will close their ears when parents lash out with a vicious tongue.

It's the fear they hear, not the voice of cheer, that once gave them courage when they walked. Their minds recall those patient words, the words that taught them how to talk.

What will it take for you to understand that all they need is that loving hand, the hand that held them and let them know that no matter what, we'll hold them up high and love them deeply forever so.

CHILDREN DO THEIR DANCE

An innocent smile with sparkling eyes, they giggle as they dance with their hands stretched towards the sky. Their minds are free and set on high, without a need to worry or even a need to cry.

Their proud parents should form pools in their gaze, for watching the children do their dance can release our pain, and to our Father, we should give Him praise.

Children are a gift from God, a special package with open arms; they hug, they tug, they kiss our cheek, they make us cry for joy, they should really make us feel weak.

For they are the special gift that God does bring, like all nature's creatures that come every year in spring.

INNOCENCE REBORN

When we take our first breath, innocence is born—a frail body and a mind still blank. We don't even know our names; they could be Bob, Bill, or Hank.

We see nothing but shadows and hear soft voices. We haven't yet learned about the wrong and right choices.

As mere children of God, it pleases Him deeply to hear the cries from one so helpless and weak. This is what God wants us to feel and seek.

Sometimes we think we'd like to be reborn and live life over again. But do we really want to face our troubles, stumble and fall, and relive our sins once more?

Who's to say it would be any different? Would we have new quests? Would we want to deviate from God's plan to become our very best?

This is the difference in growing up—to be who you are, a child, just a young little pup.

To know that there's a bright side to everything we do, we understand the need to change and not live the way we used to.

It may seem harsh at times and often too hard to handle, but if it was so easy and no problems to face, life would be dull and senseless and no reason for God's grace.

God has given us what we need. All we have to do is grow the seed, and He'll do the rest if we're willing to concede.

All God wants for us is to become our very best, to live life to its fullest extent, confess our sins, and show true repent.

But wait, God wants to enhance our lives, to change what's inside all of us, to reach the core, to let go of our pride and sin no more.

It's not about being perfect; it's about love and compassion. Some may think this is really old-fashioned.

If seeing is believing, then all we have left is a doubtful, worn-out body that will be planted in the grass.

Our spirit and beliefs are what keep us alive, guiding us to make the right choices and continue making great strides.

When we accept this fact, it can make us choke with joy. Then we'll see the happy faces of children when they play, or a newborn puppy that has just learned to bay.

Children are our future and will follow what we do. So don't use the excuse that they're weak and frail because, in truth, they can help me and you.

IN SEARCH OF MY FATHER

I'm feeling sad, for I am my father's son. Most of my life has been spent trying to decide whether to die or run, with my finger on the trigger on an imaginary gun.

I have two fathers who I've needed all my life, one who watched from afar and one who abandoned me for another wife.

Little did he know when he left that day, he took a part of me with him, not caring if I wept or strayed.

It has misguided me all my life, making me feel lost and inept, so I continued into darkness and deeper I slowly crept.

I know God watched me ruin my life; He was always there. The problem was, I didn't know He cared.

He made me strong with His name in my talk, but the problem was evident: I couldn't walk the walk.

God wanted me to carry His message with love and care, but the problem and the truth were, I wasn't sure if He was there.

When a ray of hope and a light suddenly appeared, I slowly emerged from my darkness like the massive tall trees. I felt God's instincts guiding me, like the busy buzzing bees.

I thank you, Father, for I am your love and your son. I will serve you forever, spreading love and cheer to those who are lost and the many who are unable to hear.

DON'T GIVE UP, JUST LISTEN

Blazing a new trail in the jungle of life, God gives you a new meaning to do what is right.

The blue skies, a warm heart, a strong smile—that's new for a start.

We see children laughing while grown-ups cry; the young ones sit back, watching their parents slowly die.

They, too, feel the pain that their parents emit, an endless weaving web that for themselves they have knit.

The children now run, not laughing anymore; there's just numbness where there once was a cheerful roar.

They look at the world rushing by, leaning on each other as they cry, trying to energize their souls that have run dry.

The children are giving up; they don't see any hope as they try to cope with uncertainty and fear. The outcome is too unstable for their sanity to cure.

But there is hope if we turn our eyes upon Jesus, who will lead us and show us the way today. For He is the way, the light, and we should listen to what He has to say.

I know it doesn't sound easy, and what do I mean?

What it boils down to is this… there's a list, and He wants you on it, to shake your fist at Satan and walk in the light of God, not veering from the path of righteousness, and not turning away. For in the end, for all who believe, there will be a flash of lights and a glorious array.

CHILDREN PLEASE STAY

When I hear children talk of fear and despair, it makes my heart sad and raises my hair.

My skin lights up when the Holy Spirit flows through, it tells me this to reach out to you!

Those of you who choose not to live should learn about God and what He's willing to give.

It's a relief from hopelessness and despair; He's waiting for you, He's standing right there.

Just open your heart; He knows your demise. You can't see Him, but He'll open your eyes.

He wants to embrace your soul, to make you clean, to make you whole to His Son to be seen.

So what are you waiting for, the easy way out? There is no other way but to be released from fear and doubt.

Hopelessness is the negative side; God can give you hope if you'd just drop your pride.

If you take all that energy bent on self-destruction, you won't think of your life as nothing but bad luck. Just let God into your heart, and soon you'll find that God is good and what you've been searching for all this time.

What have you got to lose? You say your life is so bad that you're willing to take that endless snooze?

God can't make your life any worse than it is, so give God a chance if you're tough enough to live.

He just wants your love, and He truly wants you to stay. It's so easy; all you have to do is truly believe and pray.

God Commands

When we feel that old sinful nature begin to rise, temptation feeds the flesh and soon strains our wandering eyes.

How can we resist when it becomes too strong? We should, because God says it's wrong!

The commands He made were meant to be obeyed, to keep our lives in line. So keep this thought and sin not, for God is good, not blind.

GOD'S LITTLE BABY

When we're born, we see shadows and hear soft voices that we can't describe. This is confusion to us, so we cry and cry.

These are new sounds that we hear, they are very foreign to our ears, because we just came from a safe place, a lukewarm feeling against our face.

Our tiny little digits grip at anything that we can, a trusting finger, a loving hand.

Even though we can't see, we know the person holding us. Our instincts form a bond, our hearts become still, like we've been touched by a wand.

Later in the years, these were gifts that we took for granted, stuffing our feelings while we ranted and raved, like a child that was lost and wanted to be saved.

We don't have to think this way anymore, just put your mind back in that space, that lukewarm feeling against your face. It's not hard to do, just call to Jesus and He'll walk you through.

He helps us remember those feelings of joy during those safe times of every little girl and boy.

Do you sense it, people? Just put your hands towards the sky. God will open your heart, and Jesus will make you sigh.

It doesn't hurt to feel safe again. Let God help you remember those lost feelings you had, those loving feelings as a young little lass or lad.

A Mother's Hope

May my mother hear no more wailing in the morning or a battle cry at noon. Praise be to the Lord that He did not take me in the womb.

Did I come into this world to bring trouble and pain and end my days in shame? Nay, I say, and I shall live to see another day!

My mother lives with hope of one day seeing her son grow, to live in peace for many days as he continues to watch the sun rise and hears the cries from the roosters when they crow.

TRY MY SHOES

When we were young and the first to arrive, we learned how to walk, and we were the apple of our parents' eyes.

We grew up and played without a care in the world. Then one day, we were told that we had a little baby brother on the way, and into a spin we were hurled.

It seemed exciting to us at the time, but when the moment came to see our little brother's eyes, we saw the love and attention he received, and we soon learned how to despise.

The love that used to be ours was held so soft and gentle in our mother's caring arms.

We lash out with mischievous pranks of hate, and soon turn into an almost fatal scene; a bottle of children's aspirin little brother has ate.

Big brother was so full of hate, but he didn't realize what this would do. His little brother was innocent, a recent gift from God to you.

Well, big brother was sent away to a home where no one cared, and his room was freezing cold and in this room, no one shared.

The selfishness had come back on him as this woman beat his hide, it was a daily thing that this woman would bring, that soon broke down his pride.

What little was left of this young one's heart soon turned into fits of rage. A red-eyed boy backed into a corner and said, "You can't do this to me anymore, and I'm not afraid!" But little did he know that as he hit the floor, this woman would have even more rage than before!

She tore the clothes from off his back and beat his privates in an endless, vicious attack!

She dragged his bleeding body across the rug to an open closet door; she threw him in and turned the key, as he laid there petrified on the heavily salted floor.

Weeks went by, and he learned not to cry, as he laid in his own vulgar mess. He was weak from starvation and so was his heart, reliving the shame for his little brother from the very start.

This woman would feed him just enough to stay alive, the only thing that was left, was just to lay down and die!

He was only three, but he had heard words about God. So, with whatever energy he had left, he called out to a God he couldn't see and confessed his wrongs for what he had done. He felt the shame, the shame for all his wrongs.

Lying naked and cold and his stomach grumbling bold, he felt God's healing hands. God filled his stomach with a touch of love and he gave him the strength to take a stand.

This gave him courage and the will to live, the will of God for this little man. He lay secure and unafraid, asking God to help him out of his deathly den. He professed to God that, no matter what, he would never do to another what had been done to him or his little brother ever again.

God answered his desperate prayer and sent a woman to relieve him of his nightmarish scare.

Well, the nightmare was gone, but the dreams lived on as he was scarred for life and continued on and on.

As the years passed on with his head tied in knots, dreams of suicide were in his thoughts.

God felt it was time to help him remember what he had forgotten. God had helped in his time of need, now it was time for him to plant God's seed.

    The story told here is of a faith too blind to see. If a mere child of three could believe in a God he couldn't see to save his life and hold his faith on just a word, then maybe, just maybe, we could become that child again, and our prayers would surely be heard. AMEN!

A Child's Love

I had a love when I was young and small; it taught me joy when I was short, not tall.

There were giggles and laughter in my carefree heart, no need for concern, for love was an art.

A beautiful scenery where soft colors flowed free, a warm soothing voice that was inside of me.

Colors and scents moved like mid-summer's breeze, the strokes of life that would capture many in moments like these.

I trusted many because I had no reason to doubt, the pictures I saw made me love, not pout.

As my mind grew in years, it became filled with hate; I saw children pointing fingers as they learned how to rate.

They rated you by the clothes that you wear, or by the color and style of your hair.

It was hard growing up, and I cried many nights, the vicious words of hate, and my direction I soon lost sight.

I couldn't share their anger, for I felt too much pain, the put-downs, the insults, I kept for my own selfish gains.

Now, many may not understand when I use the term selfish gains, but what it means is this: it allowed me to save and release vile pain, to unleash my anger in a fury of foul names.

It was an infection that boiled to the top, a fear that was growing, that I just couldn't stop.

There were memories of hurt and countless days, of names and faces, and disfigured displays.

It got to the point where I thought everyone was the same, a hate for all, and for all were the blame.

Now listen very closely to what I've got to say: if you use reason and put your own thoughts aside, you will use this lesson when you decide to drop that influential pride.

You see, the influence of others controlled my mind and covered the love I once had, it made me hate, fearing everything in my way, leaving my heart empty and sad.

It made me take and take and never show true love because people to me were just another face I could take advantage of.

The thoughts that raced through my head were eating at my soul, making me search for answers to patch my empty hole.

The answers lay deep in my past, that little giggling child that would soon come to pass.

A light switched on one day that brought back the picture I once knew, the flooding of tears for me, and especially the ones I have for you!

Yes, for you! The children of the world, the building blocks of our future, into which darkness has covered your eyes, making you see only hate, and to many, you show despise.

I know it's hard and how it feels to suffer with pain, but let loose of your fear and love everyone the same, and God will help you live, showing you endless love, from the child who knew no shame.

COOL KIDS

My life in adolescence was all about sports and guys, but I hit high school and girls had caught my eyes.

It was hard for me to fit in, for the way my life had been, so I listened to others and how they got their kicks, and their lustful stories of sin.

This intrigued my drive and my will to fit in, so I went to my parents' liquor cabinet, and my first drink was gin.

Well, I consumed half a fifth, and I was really feeling great, but the myth took its toll, and I got sick because I hadn't ate.

I was sick for three days, and I swore never again to pick up that bottle with the foul odor of gin.

But when I told the others that my spree was at an end, they turned their heads, and once again, I was without friends.

I tried to be normal and mingle with the crowd, but they laughed, they mocked, they made me blush. It wasn't long before I was looking for that rush.

That rush that made me feel like I really belonged, it made me invincible, it made me feel strong.

I was cool now and taking any drug I could find, especially the ones that made me forget, and the ones that kept me blind.

My parents soon noticed that my behavior had changed, especially my stepfather, because now I was stealing change.

It was minimal at first, and I lied when I was asked. This was no small matter, and my habit was building fast. I started bringing my cool friends around; this raised some questions and brought on some frowns.

I was soon told to stay away from the people who I thought were my friends, as my parents continued on with a frown, they said,

"These people will amount to no good, and they're taking you down."

I wouldn't listen because it was better than being abused at home, my newfound friends would never leave me alone.

I ran, and I drank, I smoked, and I cranked, I ran my life into the ground, and deeper I sank.

Then suddenly, I found I was all alone. I had run my friends off because I continued to ingest more and more of the unknown.

The cool people had all gone away, and I was the only one left who still staggered and swayed.

I didn't see it at the time, but I can see it now, that I had become who my parents had warned me about. As I look back, I'm not pleased with how I was raised, but I can look to my heavenly Father and give him all the glory and praise, for I know now it was all meant to be, for my life was a school for all to see.

A Child's True Nightmare (Part I)

As an adult, I dream every night, it seems of things I know nothing about. While I sleep everything seems so real, but when I wake I think of how I feel. There's nothing I can do, and I can't be something I'm not, this fear inside and my head tied all in knots. I dream one day of becoming the person I could have been before this all began, and lead a normal life trying to live with minimal sin.

I was so excited before going to bed. All I could think of was that my Dad was home. There were so many nights spent thinking of how the other kids teased me all day telling me how I didn't have a father and that I was a bastard child. Well, that's what their mothers had told them.

As I laid there I thought to myself, "things are going to be different from now on! At least that's what I thought until I woke the next morning in a strange place that echoed at the slightest sound.

Opening my eyes, I sat up and noticed I had been sleeping on a small mattress in the corner of the room. Looking to my right I noticed a door, it must lead out of here. I stood up and walked over standing in front of the metal door. Barely able to reach the knob, I wrapped my small hands around it and turned from side to side, but it was locked. Suddenly I felt paralyzed and very uneasy. I was totally awake now and my head was spinning, "where was I"? Suddenly this voice startled me and silenced my curiosity. "I see you are awake". I turned around shaking and asked her where my mother was and she replied that she would explain to me after she got me something to eat.

I went back to my bed in the corner and sat there motionless. A few moments later a buzzer went off and I about jumped out of my skin as the door made a clicking sound and a strange woman entered the room walking towards me with a bowl and a small carton of milk. She leaned down saying, "here you go you must be frightened. It 's okay we'll take care of you now." I started to cry while trying to choke down the cereal. "What does she mean she'll take care of me now! I want my mother to do that!"

After I had finished I sat there and all I could think of, "where was my mother?" A little while later the woman came back and picked up my bowl and led me out of the room and introduced me to another woman who was now my case worker. She said to the woman, "Is this the one"?

Looking down at me she smiled and introduced herself and showed me to her office. As she started to explain why I was there I stopped her and said, I didn't want to be there and I wanted to go home. She told me that wasn't possible and asked me if I knew what I had done. I looked at her puzzled. She said do you remember what happened with your little brother? Your Parents feel they can't control you anymore and they thought you might do more harm to your brother. I started to cry uncontrollably. She told me not to worry; she would find a good home for me.

She said there was a woman who had lost her son that was just a little bit older than me when he died. I sat there in shock not saying a word. The lady made a phone call and did some paperwork.

Gathering my things she led me out to the car and we drove for what seemed like hours deep in the woods. I remember just before we arrived we traveled a long stretch of road that followed an inlet to the bay. When we finally arrived at the house, we turned down a steep dirt driveway.

I suddenly had an eerie feeling and felt sick to my stomach. Before we could even get out of the car, I saw the front door open. This woman started walking towards the car with an odd· look on her face, half smile and half expressionless. Her smile seemed false as She walked over to my side of the car. Opening the door she said, "Is this the boy you mentioned? Well you must be hungry. It was a long drive out here wasn't it? I was terrified and didn't know what to say to her. All I could think of was the cold wet chills that were going up and down my spine. I turned to my caseworker and said I didn't want to go with her.

Something felt wrong. "Did I mention that since I can remember I've had this gift, that when I get near someone who isn't right, my gut that tells me something's is wrong?

Before my worker could reply to what I had said the woman interrupted saying this is your new home, why don't we go inside and she can get on her way. I'm sure she's really busy, aren't you? Well I do have a long drive back. John, you need to go with her now, I'll call you in a couple of days to see how you're doing okay? I stood there in the driveway as I watched my worker drive away. She reached down and grabbed me by the hap.d and said let's go inside and get you something to eat as she led me into the house.

Inside she immediately wanted to give me a tour of the house and explicitly point out the areas that were off limits. She started in the kitchen that was off limits. Down the hall to the where I saw a man laughing while watching T.V., off limits. She led me back towards the living room, which was off limits. She walked towards the staircase and led me to the top. We rounded the corner to the right. There were two rooms, one to the left and one straight ahead that had many toys.

I thought to myself, this doesnt look too bad. I asked the woman if that was my room and she replied,"no that belonged.to my Son who died, that room is only for good little boys." I replied, rm a good little boy". As she was unlocking the door she mentioned how she new what had happened to my little brother and that this would be my new home from now on. She opened the door all the way and I felt the rush of freezing cold air as it swept by my face.

Now you have to imagine, it was just after Christmas and the elevation was high and there was still a little snow on the ground. I glanced around the room seeing only a bed and dresser. I asked her where the toys were and she reminded me that bad little boys dont get to play with toys. I asked her where my clothes were and she told me all the clothes I would need were in the dresser right over there, which she took me over to and showed me. Inside the second drawer were two pairs of pants, two socks, and two shirts.

Taking one of the sets out she told me to take off the clothes I had on because they were dirty. I told her they were clean and she said, "dont argue with me, just do it! She stood there without saying a word as I changed. When I finished she told me to help her make my bed. I told her I didn't know how. She replied she would show me how and that from now on I would be making my own bed.

When we finished I told her that I was hungry. She told me that I had my chance when I was downstairs, so now I could wait until dinner. It was roughly sometime afternoon, and waiting until dinner would seem like an eternity to a three year old child. She left the room shutting the door behind her as she locked it. I stood there confused for a moment, "did she just lock me in here"? Suddenly fear set in and a feeling came over me like never before, it almost choked me! I ran for the door frantically pulling on the knob screaming for her to let me out! She came back in as I stepped back out of the way of the door as it flew open. Her stare was heartless. She told me she would leave the door open if I didn't leave the room. I told her I wouldn't. Then she turned and left leaving me feeling isolated from the whole house. I turned and walked to the many paned windows and stared aimlessly outside.

In the backyard there was an old rusty swing set and the lawn looked like it hadn't been mowed in years. I did mention it was winter, I was soon feeling the effects of this cold room. I looked around to see if there were any heating vents to nestle up to like I had at home, but I couldn't find one. How was I to stay warm? Even with my jacket on I began to shake uncontrollably from the :freezing temperature in the room. I looked over at the open door . and remembered what the woman had said about leaving the room.

At this point I didn't care, I was cold! I could see ice crystals coming from the hallway that almost looked like smoke as the warm air mixed with the cold. I knew I'd be alot warmer if I just crossed that line. I walked closer to the hall listening for any movement. As I got closer I could smell food cooking and I could hear her asking her Husband what he wanted to drink with his lunch. Hearing that and the smell of food made my stomach growl. I knew she would be busy for a little while so I stepped into the hallway. It sent shivers up my spine as I wrapped my arms around myself rubbing my arms together gaining my circulation back. I was very bold for my age, so I decided to take a chance. Maybe the man downstairs would be sympathetic to my situation. I cautiously made my way down the stairs trying not to draw attention. It was lucky for me that the kitchen door was closed as I rounded the staircase and went down the hall to the den. I heard the man laughing at a television program. I could see the back of the man's head above the chair.

When I stepped closer, the man caught me out of the corner of his eye and said, "I don't think you're supposed to be down here, you better get back upstairs before she catches you". I told him it was too cold up there, besides I would like to watch some television with you. He told me that I wasn't supposed to watch any t.v. I told him he was the man of the house, he could tell her to let me. He said she was in charge of me and went back to watching his program. I stood there continuing to watch t. v. until I heard the woman walk up behind me with her husband's lunch in her hand and with a stern voice she said," I told you this room was off limits!

    I tried to sound very sincere as I humbly told her it was too cold up there, besides I heard the t.v. and my mother would always let me watch it. She took me by the hand and briskly led me upstairs. In the room she warned me to never do that again as she was closing the door locking it behind her.

    I may have only been three years old, but I had the heart of a lion and I was mad now! My mother had talked to me like an adult, not as a child with goo-goo baby talk and I quickly learned to ask for what I wanted with the attitude of an eight year old. Fuming, I went to the window staring into the big backyard that truly had enough room for plenty of children to play in. I wondered why I couldnt at least go outside and play. At Least I wouldn't be bothering her.

    After a while the cold room began to take its toll on me again. Not only from the cold, but from uncertainty and fear. I looked over at my bed and warm thoughts ran through my head as I thought to myself; if I can't go outside and I didnt have anything to do, I might as well be warm and get some rest at the same time. I would find out later that would be a big mistake. Sleeping very peacefully I was suddenly awakened. It felt like I'd not even go to sleep. It was not a very pleasant sight waking up to this woman yanking me out of bed screaming at me for sleeping under the covers with my clothes on.

She said that I had dirtied the sheets and that I would have to make the bed all over again. At three this was a very difficult task. I felt helpless doing what my mother had always done for me. When I had finished, she told me to never sleep under the covers with my clothes again, and that sleeping in the bed was only for night time.

Well, most children would be happy not having to take a nap, but in this situation I was welcoming being able to sleep since there wasn't anything else to do. I was offended by her actions and of course I had to say something. Taking a stand I told her she couldnt treat me like this. I went on telling her how my mother never made me make my bed and that I always took a nap in the afternoon. This is when reality set in and hit me like a damp moldy rag that had been thrown in my face. She told me that I might as well forget all about what my mother used to do, because she didn't want me anymore. She went on to say that the state pays them to take care of me and that she could do anything she wanted and that I'd better get used to it.

This didn't sit very well with me and I began to scream at her to let me go outside and play! She came closer towering over me as I looked up at her with no fear.... at this time. She just looked at me, then turned away walking out the door and of course locking it behind her. I felt furious but

mostly frustrated at this point and now feeling a lot of anger towards my mother.

Questions began running through my head, "why had my mother done this to me, why was I even here, I didn't mean to give all those childrens aspirins to my little brother, they tasted like candy. I started pacing awkwardly. Then I stopped as I heard heavy footsteps coming upstairs. I stood there motionless.

Then the woman unlocked the door and walked in the room

with a belt in her hand and told me to remove my clothes. I told her I didn't want to, it was too cold in here. I looked at the belt having no idea what it was for because I had never had one used on me, but I was about to find out. She put down the belt and began to remove my clothing. Now naked, I covered my privates in shame because I didn't know this woman. I never did this in front of my mother, but this woman was a stranger.

She stood by my side staring at me. Then without warning, "WACK", the belt caught me across the face. I covered my face in sheer pain! Then again, "WACK", this time she hit my privates! I had never felt pain like this before! My head exploded in horrifying gestures as I dropped to my knees trying to cover all the areas of my body she was hitting, but I couldn't, the lashes were coming at me too fast. suddenly a blinding flash of light. The belt had found my face again, this time closing one eye. I rolled on the cold tile floor with one hand on my privates and the other covering my face as I felt the belt attacking me over and over unmercifully. When she had finished she told me to stand up. I couldn't, I was choking and crying uncontrollably and shaking from the cold floor. She then stood me up and threw my clothes at me and said to get dressed or I would get some more. Well I didn't want that, so I began putting my clothes on. I could feel the hot welts burning as I dragged them across my swollen privates and I started to cry. Raising the belt she told me to stop crying or I would get some more! I barely held back the tears because I didn't want to ever experience that again.

When I was dressed she said not to go near the bed until I was told. She then walked out and locked the door. I began to cry into my arms so she wouldn't hear me. My head was about to explode from rage and terror. The shock was beginning to wear off and I was feeling the ill effects from the beating. I had extreme pain all over, but mostly coming from my privates.

I carefully pulled down my pants. I stared at my swollen privates that were bleeding and secretions oozing from the welts. The cool air made it feel a little better. It hurt to barely touch it, so I left my pants undone letting the cold air ease the pain. I turned to stare out the window and my mind went blank as I was still in shock from the whole ordeal.

The hair stood on the back of my neck as I realed around when I heard the woman coming back upstairs. I quickly fastened my pants so she wouldn't find me like this and beat me again. She opened the door and just looked at me. Without saying a word, she then closed the door. My adrenaline surging through my body allowed me not to feel the pain from my tight pants, but that soon wore off and brought on tears of agony. I felt so lonely thinking to myself, "what did I do that was so terrible? It hurt to much to stand, so I laid down on the floor and screamed in my head as the tears flowed down my cheeks thinking, "how could my mother have done this to me? Why did she hate me so much to put me here with this woman? This I believe is when I began to hate myself and everyone else. I laid there curled in a fetal position petrified choking on my own secretions, unable to crawl away from a perplexing situation. My crying soon subsided as I laid there feeling worthless letting my mind soothe my aching soul. Some time had passed and my body rudely woke me shaking from the freezing floor.

I sat up wrapping my arms around my convulsing body staring at the bed that looked so inviting. I was very apprehensive, do I dare? Warm thoughts suddenly made the fear go away. I thought to myself, "if I just lay on top she wouldn't know the difference. I could just jump up before she came into the room.

I stood up slowly feeling my clothes pulling away from the sticky welts. I walked over to the bed and laid down. It felt cold, but it soon warmed up after a few minutes, and it was better than the cold tile floor. I soon fell asleep. Fear must have made my senses sharp, because I woke just as I heard the keys. I was on my feet before she could get the door open. I stood there innocently not saying a word. She asked me if I was hungry, of course I was, as I nodded my head yes in response. She turned away and went back downstairs, surprisingly she left the door open. I could see the ice crystals in the air forming from the warm air mixed from my freezing room. I walked over to the door and extended my arm into the hallway. Feeling the warmth sent shivers throughout my whole body.

I ventured further absorbed by the hypnotic affect the heat had on my better judgment. The warmth sharpened my senses. This pleasing feeling quickly disappeared as fast as it came when I heard the woman coming back upstairs. I rushed back to my bedside feeling my stomach growling from hunger. I hadn't eaten all day and for a child that was an eternity. When she entered the room my eyes widened when I saw the sandwich and glass of milk. She allowed me to sit in the bed when I ate. My first bite made me salivate, I could taste the peanut butter and jelly, after that the rest of the sandwich was a blur. She watched me as I ate. When I had finished I asked for more, she said I had had enough, but my stomach told me differently. She then took my dishes leaving the room and of course locking the door. I sat there for a moment reliving the peanut butter and jelly sandwich.

It didn't take long for the sugar to kick in and I was soon trying to find something to occupy my energetic young body. There wasn't anything in the room to play with. The only thing I had to keep my attention was the gloomy view outside from my glass cage. I call it that because there were windows that covered three quarters of the room. I stared at the many panes of glass and began to count them from the left to right. Since I could only count to ten, I did it over and over. The count came to five tens plus eight. When I was bored with that, I began pacing the room back and forth counting the tiles on the floor. I can't remember how many times I did that but it was growing dark and I was getting hungry again. Darkness soon blanketed the night as I stood there staring at my reflection from the light in the room for the longest time, crying whenever I thought about my mother.

I was becoming very depressed at what was happening to me. I tried to remember the night before when my parents dropped me off at the place I left this morning, but I couldn't even remember seeing their faces. To this day Itlstill not sure who took me there, neither one of them will admit it, they both point the finger at each other. They just say," let it go John, it's all in the past, it will go away if you just let it go.

Well, my legs were getting tired, so I sat on the floor and fell asleep. I woke to the sound of keys again. As the door opened up I expected to see the woman, but it was her husband. He was holding a plate of food in his hand. I could smell it as soon as he walked in, it was roast beef with mashed potatoes and gravy. He sat the plate on the nightstand. I could also see corn and a roll which made me shake with anticipation. He walked out the door without a word and left the door wide open which made me feel a little more comfortable. I devoured my plate in record time. With my plate licked clean, I stood at the door calling out for seconds as I was used to asking for more. I called several times until her husband finally came upstairs. I stood there with my plate in hand asking for more. He said; "My wife said there isn't anymore, and that would have to do me until the morning".

Of course I was disappointed, but at least I wasn't starving. He started to close the door and I jumped up asking him not to. He hesitated for a moment and said, "okay, just don't leave the room".

Not having anything to do, I went back to staring out the window. I don't know why, all I could see was my reflection. Without anything to do, I laid on the floor and tried to sleep, but I couldnt. I could hear the T.V. downstairs along with both of them laughing while I laid there torn between my former home and the nightmare that was about to begin. My attention was diverted when I heard someone coming upstairs. I didn't know who it was so I quickly rose to my feet not wanting to get caught supposedly doing something wrong. It must be time to go to bed as the husband walked in carrying a package of brand new pajamas which he started opening as he told me to get undressed for bed. As I started he could see that I was having trouble, not because I didn't know how, because the welts hurt as the clothes dragged over the lightly scabbed wounds.

Helping me undress he never said a word about the welts that were everywhere, he carefully slipped the warm cotton pajamas over my numb frail body. The pajamas felt so good against my icy flesh. After all that had happened that day I felt compelled to ask him one more time if l could watch some t.v. He said he would ask his wife, she was the one that was in charge of me.

He stood at the door and called down to her. Her response was no! I looked up at him and reminded him of his gender and said, "you're the man of the house, you could tell her to let me, couldn't you"? No, she brought you into this house so she is responsible for letting you do anything. I became silent and confused. I thought to myself, "she is in control! This meant I was in serious trouble, because no matter how much I wanted all this to go away, it could only get worse. She made that perfectly clear when she said I was a bad little boy. The man motioned me towards the bed and said that he would tuck me in.

When he finished, I watched as he started to close the door behind him. I said," please don't close the door. He looked at me and said sorry as the door softly shut and locked it as it closed. I laid there for a few minutes as I felt the cold slowly place its frosty mits on the tip of my nose. I pulled the covers over my head and fell fast asleep.

The next morning I woke up with my eyes all fuzzy and saw a shadowy figure standing in front of me. I called out, "mommy? My eyes soon cleared and startled me for a moment when I saw it was the woman standing there with a breakfast tray in her hand. I realized all that happened wasn't a dream and fear set in; but the overwhelming smell of oatmeal and toast made me sit upright. I hesitated for a moment when she leaned down placing the tray in my lap.

She seemed different, actually pleasant. She watched me as I ate. When I finished, she picked up my tray. She stood there for a moment just staring at me, then turned as the door closed behind her hearing the key turn. I felt so powerless as I sat in this cold empty room. So much space and only a bed and dresser to fill this gloomy place. Crawling out of bed, I jumped back up when my feet touched the floor sending cold shock waves immediately to my brain telling me, "that was cold"! I am awake now! This time I slowly placed my feet on the floor letting my body absorb the cold gradually. I walked over to the window and stood there motionless staring into the desolate backyard.

I began pacing back and forth wishing I was outside playing like l normally was at this time of the morning. I stopped for a moment noticing the chill in the room as I blew smoke from my freezing breath. Between the arctic temperature in the room and nothing to do I was getting mad and I'd only been awake for a short time. I decided to get dressed since I was freezing. I removed my top feeling the brisk air clench my tight body as my breathing quickened, so did my pace. I sat up on my bed to put my shoes and socks on.

By the time I was fully dressed, the rage was beginning to well up inside me. I had had enough! Keeping me in this cold room and nothing to play with! I stomped my feet screaming with blinding fury as I started ripping the sheets off the bed! Still screaming, my face turning red with furious contempt for this woman. Emaged, and thinking over and over, "no one can treat me this way, keeping me caged like an animal"! My mind went blank as I continued stripping my bed, throwing them on the floor, kicking at them with sheer vengeance. In all my anger I didn't hear her come through the door until I felt the warm air and the door hitting the wall. I was startled when she turned me around and told me to put the sheets back on the bed. She recanted by saying, "no, better yet, make your bed"! I told her that the sheets were dirty from the floor. She said that I got them dirty, so I would be sleeping in them tonight.

In all the confusion, I hadn't noticed the belt in her hand:t I was having trouble with the second sheet so she put down the belt and helped me finish. When she was done she picked up the belt and told me to remove my clothes. I stared at the belt and did not argue with her thinking she would take it easier on me this time. I stood there looking up at her naked again. I started to shake not just from the cold room, but from her face that was slowly changing, almost demon possessed. Her eyes deepened, almost red when she raised the belt. I covered my privates, but that wasn't her first mark. She un-yielded vicious strikes from my head to my feet. I did everything I could to keep her from hitting my privates, but it wasn't enough. Then it was over. When she stopped,-she just left the room leaving me lying there curled in a ball crying in pain and fear from a hopeless situation. She didn't even bother to make me dress this time. After some time I got dressed out of necessity; I was freezing! When I finished raking my clothes across my hot welts, I laid back down on the floor. I must have been in shock, because I couldn't really feel the welts, not yet.

This became a daily ritual. I can't remember how long it was before I quit cowering and stood my ground once more. This particular morning she came in and woke me with," her soft voice". In my mind I questioned her motives when she handed me my usual oatmeal and toast. I never complained about the food she gave me. I wasn't starving, at least not yet! I felt my courage welling inside me to challenge her methods of madness.

As I finished my last bite, she immediately took the tray from my lap and set it down saying, "allright it's time". I thought to myself, "time for what?" Her voice sounded so nice, I had no idea what she was talking about. I looked at her and said, "Do I get to go outside?" She reached for the nightstand, then I knew what she meant. Yanking me out of bed, she stood there with the belt. I didn't understand, I hadn't talked back to her, I just woke up! She never beat me this early.

Her voice changed suddenly as she sternly told me to remove my pajamas. I stood there defiantly and said, "No, you can't do this to me anymore, I didn't do anything wrong!" She was enraged!

She grabbed me, throwing me to the floor and literally ripping my clothes off. I felt the coller tighten around my neck as she tried pulling my top off from behind. She flipped me over, tearing at the snaps as she removed my top. Then she yanked my bottoms off, leaving the lower part of my body hanging in mid-air and slamming to the freezing floor. She stood me up, grabbing my hands and holding them above my head. Dangling in the air sideways, I saw her arm go back with the belt. Inflamed, she began beating my privates over and over and over until I couldn't feel the pain anymore. I couldn't even hear the sound of her voice. All I could see was the belt hacking away at my waist and her distorted mouth moving in violent gestures. I remember falling to the floor as she let me go. I laid there for what seemed like an eternity, my mind was numb.

Slowly I began to hear her voice, "I told you to get up, now get up!" I couldn't move. I felt my body convulsing from the shock it had received. I didn't know what to do. My body was jerking uncontrollably, I couldn't function! I tried to move as she kept screaming at me to get up! She thought I was ignoring her, but I really couldn't move!

In her rage to my defiance, she reached down and grabbed me by the hair spinning me around twisting my skin on the tile and began to drag me across the floor towards the door. The friction was unbearable. My previous wounds and my new ones hurt deeper than before. I cried out telling her I would get up, but that was cut short when my body made contact with the hallway rug cutting into me like sandpaper! I felt my body scream and my eyes witnessed a blinding flash of light from the searing pain that the rug was inflicting.

It was a constant motion across my open welts as I flopped around trying to keep the rug from my body. Then she stopped. I laid there looking up at her. As a child I could never imagine such pain and why? I didn't see the door as it swung open slamming against my head. She pushed me out of the way with her foot, then picked me up by the arm and tossed me inside the closet slamming the door shut.

Then, I heard the lock turn and my emotions lost all control as I cried in the darkness. With my arms wrapped tightly around my legs and my head tucked between my knees I cried so hard my eyes were so swollen I could hardly see. Sitting there for hours I started to feel cramped so I made an attempt to stand. When I tried to move, pain shot throughout my whole body. It felt as if my skin was literally being torn from my back. The blood and secretion from the open welts had stuck to the wall, so the only thing I could do was lean back against the wall and try to figure out how I was going to stand. After a while I found if I did it real slow it wasn't so bad; not good mind you, but easier.

Once I had accomplished this I had another problem, my buttocks also adhered to the floor. This was much worse, because the area around my waist front and back had taken the brunt of the burden. When I tried to shift from side to side the pain from my privates intensified. They hurt so bad I felt a need to feel how damaged they were. I felt terrified when I touched them. They were so swollen they didn't even seem like they belonged to me! I felt sticky slime all over my sensitive area. I had to imagine it was blood. So I put my hand towards the light coming from the gap under the door, and I was right, it was blood! I began to cry, feeling sick to my stomach all at once, because I knew I was really hurt this time.

My body started to sweat thinking about my wounds and I began to tremble trying to imagine what was going to happen to me next. I knew I wasn't getting out of here too soon, so I needed to get comfortable. I couldn't remain sitting like this for the duration, so I slowly leaned to one side feeling my skin remain on the floor.

My whole body felt like it was on fire, from my face all the way to my feet. No matter what part I touched it hurt! After rocking from side to side again, I was able to break free. I stood feeling my wounds tighten. I was uncertain if I was going to be able to sit again, but eventually I would have to. I leaned back slowly feeling the cold wall ease my burning welts. It felt like a quick dip into a freshly filled wading pool on a hot summer's day. But it soon subsided, I was okay just as long as I didnt move. I was tired, my body needed time to heal, that meant I needed sleep. So I tried sleeping standing up, but every time I started to fall asleep, my body jerked away from the wall extracting the dried secretions that remained stuck to the wall.

This obviously wasn't working, I knew I had to lye down. When I started to squat towards the floor, I felt the welts on my legs and buttocks tear open releasing secretions and of course the pain all over again. I tried going to my knees, this helped me position myself to roll on my side. It hurt so good as I touched the cold wooden floor. It seemed like it took forever to get on my back. I had to move faster, the welts on my side were starting to stick. So in one quick motion I rolled to my back. My hot body spasamed when I came flush with the floor. "Oh but it felt so good". This was very soothing to my wounds. It didn't take long before my young mind shut down and I fell asleep.

It must have been sometime early evening, it had to be, because it was still light outside. I suddenly felt the urge to go to the bathroom as do most people do when they first wake up. My first reaction was to sit up and pound on the door to let me out, but I had one problem, I was really stuck to the floor this time. It had been hours since I'd moved and my bodily fluids had joined with the floor. When I tried to move it felt like I was glued to the surface. I had to do something fast, I was about to urinate all over myself In one motion I lurched forward feeling my skin remain on the floor.

    Once again my skin was on fire and my head was lit with blinding lights. I had to keep going while the pain was still there so I shot forward all the way this time. I was almost there when I realized that my buttocks were stuck so bad I could hardly break free. Standing to my feet I could feel and hear my wounds split and crack. The pain was so intense I don't think there are enough words in the dictionary to fully describe it. I know you're thinking how could he hear his welts cracking? Well I could and I could also feel fluids oozing down my body. I stood there ridgid trying to hold it in as I quietly knocked at first. I listened for a moment; nothing. I had to get her attention quickly, I was about to go all over the floor.

    I started pounding on the door violently, this time she heard me. I heard the keys jingling on the other side. I stood back as she unlocked the door. I thought to myself, "how did she come up the stairs without me hearing her?" She must have been standing out there the whole time. Without any expression she said,"what do you want? I told her I had to go to the bathroom. She said, "Okay; but you had better have to go"! I walked past her naked towards the bathroom. I stood in front of the toilet and tried to get up on the seat but she stopped me and said, "Oh no you don't, you're not going to get my clean toilet seat all messy, you just stand there and go!"

    I now had a problem. Number one, the toilet was too high so I had to reach for my privates to elevate it to go over the rim; but I couldn't even touch it because the pain was unbearable. Number two; I was used to sitting on the toilet to go, so I was in quite a spot. She thought I was stalling and grabbed me by the arm escorting me back to the closet. I stood there trying to convince her that I really had to go, but she didn't believe me. Just before she closed the door, she told me that if I went to the bathroom in this closet that she would beat me again. Then she shut the door and locked it. I stood there for a few minutes, then it happened. I felt the sensation come on; I had to go right now!I pounded on the door wildly begging for her to let me out, but she wouldn't listen.

At this point I didn't care. I knelt in agony as close to the corner as I could and let it go. I won't describe the sensation, but it was a relief I felt it travel past my legs. I was hoping it would leave me enough room to at least lie down. When I.had finished I had to feel around on the floor to see where it was dry and how far it had traveled. When I figured out where I could lie down, I wiped off the urine I had got on my hands on my legs, that was a mistake. The salt from my urine found an open wound and sent searing waves throughout my whole body.

I sat there for a while as the pain slowly went away, as I was afraid to lie down for the fear of the pain returning. So I tried sleeping and sitting up. This worked for a little while, but it was no use. I would just keep waking up. This was no good, I had to lie down. So I backed up all the way to the wall and pivoted my buttocks lifting my legs at the same time avoiding my mess. It hurt alot, but the outcome was going to be rewarding. Rolling on my side took the longest because my welts were opening and causing great discomfort as the they came in contact with the floor. I finally managed to stretch completely out.

The whole ordeal had drained me mentally and physically, all wanted to do was sleep. I don't know how long I was out, it seemed like I had just closed my eyes when I was startled by the woman screaming at me, "You little bastard, you peed in here just to make me mad didn't you? I gave you the chance to go to the bathroom and you waited to go in here"? She reached down and yanked me up off the floor tearing the skin off my backside and I started screaming! Without a care to the agony I was in she led me by the hand to my room which was still freezing cold and locked the door leaving me standing there naked. After a few minutes I had to admit that the cold air was making the pain go away, but the fear was still there as I heard her cursing me while she cleaned the closet floor. I slowly began backing myself into the corner awaiting the outcome. I wrapped my arms around my shaking body as I became terrified when I heard her finish.

When she entered the room she had the belt in one hand and the keys in the other. Dropping the keys to the floor she walked over and grabbed me by the arm and led me towards the bathroom. She stood me in front of the toilet and told me to go to the bathroom. No one haso.wB Idea how bad I wanted to go right now, but I had already gone and I was scared out of my mind. If I couldn't go, I can't even imagine what she would do to me. I looked up at her shaking and told her I couldn't go. She said,"you better have to go"! I looked at the toilet that was already too high for me to reach, even if I could go to go to the bathroom, I was too scared. Without any warning the belt caught the back of my legs as I jumped in the air in sheer agony.

I tried covering myself with my arms but it was no good, she was coming at me like an olympic swimmer. She took me by the arm, beating all the way back to the closet, throwing me inside and looked the door. I stood there in darkness for the longest time, afraid to move with terror racing through my young mind. My body was on fire from the new welts and also the old ones that were now re-opened.

After the initial shock wore off I noticed an odd smell in the closet and I noticed the floor was wet under my feet. Still aching I slowly bent down and ran my hand across the floor getting the wet substance on my hand. Bringing my hand up to my face I smelled the slimy liquid as my head recoiled back from the pungent smell. From my previous experience with wiping any liquid off my hands onto my body I decided to wipe it on the wall and avoid any contact with my skin. It was some time before I could manage to make it to the floor but eventually I had to. Fatigued, I slowly inched my way to the floor. I didn't have any welts directly on my knees and it felt good to rest my legs for a moment. I turned slightly to the right, extending both arms to the floor and started to roll on my side. It was but a couple of seconds after that, my wounds came in contact with the almost dry liquid.

The pain wasted no time making me lurch to my feet screaming in excruciating agony. At the time I didn't know what the liquid was, but I am telling you, this story I can smell it like it was yesterday; it was bleach! I thought the beatings were beyond reproach, they were nothing compared to bleach saturating my open wounds. Adding to the pain was the sudden jolt to my feet as I cried choking on my tears. Backing into the corner I stood there with my eyes bulging and my body in rigor. I began fanning my side trying to put out the fire but it still kept burning. I thought back on how the cold floor soothed my welts so I raised my arm above my head and slowly pressed my side against the wall. It took a couple of tries but I finally succeeded in getting some relief. I didnt ever want to sit down again, but after a considerable amount of time I had to do something.

I slowly bent down as my wounds split open once more, fatigue overriding the pain. I felt the floor, it had finally dried. I could still smell the bleach, but I was stretched to the limit.and I had to get some sleep. I tried laying on my side but the smell of the bleach was filling my nostrils. So, with what energy I had left I slowly worked my way onto my back stinging slightly from the floor. The cool floor soon put me fast to sleep. I had intermittent bursts of sleep, always waking to the light coming from under the door. I woke later and I knew the day was ending, as the light was. growing dim.

Night was setting and I was hungry and totally exhausted. I thought to myself, "there's no use going on, I give up. I remember dozing off into a deep sleep. I believe my mind and body shut down in a healing process, because I didn't wake up until some time the next morning. The smell of bacon and eggs tantilized my stomach and opened my eyes. I went to sit up, but I couldn't, I was stuck to the floor again! All the fear that had gone away in a peaceful sleep had returned tenfold. My heart was pounding and I was unable to move, I really was trapped this time.

Suddenly I felt sick to my stomach, I had to pee! I knew it would take too long to break away from the floor. So I reached for my privates putting the tenderness to the side as I aimed to the left, but I thought to myself, "If I do it in that direction I'll get it all over myself. I had to act quickly". I didn't even feel the pain as I thrusted my hips upwards. I shifted my hips twisting to the right on the unforgiving floor sending bolts of lighting through my brain, I didn't care, I was desperate. I slightly touched my privates because they were still inflamed yet scabbed over. I did my best to aim in the direction of the corner and began to relieve myself. I did manage to get some on my waste towards the end but it was minimal compared to what could have happened. Suddenly I was overwhelmed.

I felt the urine running up against my body. Now cold, it began to encompass my right side. I frantically tried detaching myself from the floor, slowly at first, but when 1 felt the urine seep into my scabless wounds fear overrode the intense pain. I realized pumping and my body ridgid, I quickly stood to my feet. Now wide awake, I realized my situation just got worse. What do I do now?

Even though I was satisfied I couldn't call out to the woman because she would see the urine and beat me again. So I stood for hours not saying a word as I ran through the nightmare. through my head over and over from the day before, what had I done that was so terrible that I deserved this? My thoughts were seemingly normal, but now they were beginning to turn into a ghastly reality.

A three year old should not be thinking these kinds of thoughts, but I was changing. I was becoming infuriated to the point it was almost hypnotic with sadistic thoughts of what I might do to this woman if I were her size! As the day dragged on I tortured myself reliving the events over and over continually asking myself, Why did my mother hate me so to put me with this woman? Throughout the day I periodically checked the floor to see if it was dry. Finally some time in the afternoon it was safe to lie down and I was so relieved because my legs didn't have much strength left. As I layed down I was starving because this was the second day without food and I was uncertain of the outcome and death had not entered the picture yet.

At the end of the day I was so hungry I began tapping on the door lightly hoping she would see that I was being docile and have pity on me so she would give me something to eat. I was helpless and at her mercy. The only thing different about laying there naked than being in my room, I wasn't freezing.

Nighttime was settling in and the smell of dinner had my mind in an uproar! Having crazed from the lack of food for days, I started pounding on the door to get her attention, or for her to at least acknowledge that I was still in the closet. In all my hysterical attempts she still didn't answer. Has she forgotten about me? I listened to every sound in the house, it was the only thing I had to occupy my time. I listened to her as she finished her meal and started on the dishes. I knew it was no use as I saw the lights go out and I was in total darkness. It was time to rest as I positioned myself on my back hearing my wounds crack trying to find a comfortable posture. Putting my feet against the wall took the pressure off my beaten legs. It didn't hurt for very long as I was learning how to numb this momentary discomfort. I turned my head towards the gap under the door, the light began to get brighter as the cloud cover disappeared and the moon was out giving me a bit of hope, a spark of life to hang onto. I soon fell asleep, but the true nightmares were just beginning. I was in a deep sleep when I was awakened from something brushing against my arm. I opened my eyes and tried to focus. The light from the moon showed a silhouette of a small creature of some sort. I was excited!

Finally I had something to fill my void of loneliness. I stretched out my hand in friendship trying to coax it closer so I could see, so I could be intimate with something. I watched it as it crept cautiously closer. Its nose touched my hand and I returned the favor by trying to pet it. I stroked it, feeling the fur on its back. Then without warning it bit me! I panicked, ripping myself from the floor and recoiling into the corner. Frightened I wondered, "Why did it bite me, where did it go, would it bite me again? I sat in the corner paralyzed trying to focus on the light, attempting to catch a glimpse of its shadow.

Then I saw it. It was a big rat! I sat cowardly trying to cover my vulnerable parts, but I couldn't protect them all. I watched as it crawled under the door and into the house. I waited for what seemed like an eternity. Ultimately the rat returned, stopping to gaze at me in the darkness with its red glowing eyes. I listened as I heard it crawl back into its hole. I waited for a while before I decided to lay back down. I know it was quite some time before I was able to go back to sleep.

This went on for so many days I stopped counting. I watched the light under the door rise and fall from sunrise to sunset whenever I was awake, and the moon whenever the clouds were not present; of course, the rat had his nightly routine and I didnt sleep until it was done with his rounds. By this time I was laying in both excrements as I finally had to go number two, but I believe that was all I had left in me. I was pretty much used to the smell since I was around it twenty four hours a day. I was becoming deranged, making up pretend kids to play with and talking to them on a regular basis. I didn't even laugh while I played with them as most children do, but there was no humor where my mind was taking me.

One day when I couldn't sleep I heard a encouraging sound, the woman was coming upstairs. She opened the door with a disgusting look on her face and said, " You filthy little animal!

I just stared at her petrified not knowing what she would do at this point.

So, I made an attempt at reconciliation by telling her that I was sorry and I'll be good from now on. She didn't say a word until I asked her if I could get out of the closet. She said, "You had your chance, now you will live like the animal that you are". She turned and walked downstairs leaving the door open. It felt good feeling the warm air caress my bare flesh. I think. She was hoping that I would come out of the closet so she could have an excuse to beat me again, but I didn't dare move from my spot, I'll show her, I'm not moving!

A moment later she came back upstairs and said, "here", as she handed me a half peanut butter sandwich and a half glass of water. I devoured it, drooling the whole fifteen seconds that it took me to eat it. When I was finished she took the plate and glass and shut the door locking it. Alone once again, my madness called out to my imaginary friends, I was really losing it. I mean I could actually see them and carry on a conversation, I was slowly going insane. Feeling worthless and cold, the day was at an end. Darkness grew nearer, smelling dinner and listening to my stomach grumble and the sounds of empty pots and pans. The lights finally went out and I knew what time it was. The rat would soon be coming out of its hole and going on its nightly raid.

I would have to wait lengthy periods of time before the rat would return and I could go back to sleep, but it was always a restless slumber anyway. The only time I really had any uninterrupted sleep was during the day time. This one particular morning I woke up weaker than the previous days and felt defeated. I would usually wait for her to bring me my half a sandwich and water, but today I thought to myself, "what's the use?", so I just went back to sleep. Some time later I opened my eyes to the sound of a man's voice coming upstairs. It was her husband saying, " Where is he?" and she replied, "He's in the closet".

My demented mind thought he was coming to finish me off since he had done nothing to stop this insanity. He opened the door and I remember seeing the shocked look on his face and what he said to his wife. "My God what have you done to him?"

He went to reach down for me and I quickly sat up backing into the corner. He said, "Don't be afraid, I'm not going to hurt you".

When he picked me up in his arms I saw the look on the woman's face when he told her to clean up the mess while he gave me a bath. He took me to the bathroom and I stood there as he drew my bath water. I was hesitant to trust him as I thought, "How could he let her do this to me?" Setting me down in the tub, I jumped up when the warm water found my injured privates that were still sensitive even though they were scabbed over. He said he was sorry and let me stand as he gently ran the wash rag over all the tender areas. His

soothing voice made me feel I could trust him when he asked me what she had done. I cried while trying to tell him all the peticulars, but my young soul had been broken to the point of hysteria and I couldn't finish. I wanted to, but the cruelty I had endured choked my thoughts.

He hugged my wet body trying to comfort my weary mind telling me he had no idea she was doing this. He told me that he would make sure she would never do this again. When my crying had ceased, I looked at him and said, "How come you let her do this to me?" He said, "I didn't know, you see, I drive a big truck, that's how I make my living and I'm gone for weeks at a time; but, I promise you, it won't happen again".

A warm feeling ran over me, he saved my life and I felt grateful as I started to cry feeling comfort in his words.

After he was done bathing me, he took me to my room and helped me dress, being careful not to re-open my seabed body. My clothes felt foreign and their warmth eased any fear that I had left. He then left for a moment and said that he would be right back. When he returned he had an arm full of toys that he had gotten from his dead son's room. My eyes widened when he set them down on the bed. I was so excited I didn't know what to do. He told me they were his sons and that he wanted me to have them. He smiled at me before he turned and left the room. Inquisitive, I asked him if I could see his truck. He turned and hesitated for a moment, then said, "Sure, as he reached down and picked me up and said it was right outside. Taking me downstairs he opened the front door and my eyes darted in all directions absorbing everything in their path.

The fresh air filled my lungs as I inhaled the crisp morning dew. It was misty out and the birds chattered with their morning conversations. Then there it was. It was big as a house. I don't remember what color it was, but its chrome glistened from a recent wash. He opened the cab door, then took me up these giant steps as he grabbed the rail beside the door and put me on the seat. Then he told me to sit on the engine cover as he climbed inside.

I remember the loud buzzing sound it made as he turned the key, then he pushed a button and started the roaring diesel. It was so loud I could hardly hear while the door was open so I covered my ears. He looked at me laughing saying, "Too loud for you?, here let me close the door. When the door closed it was much quieter. I felt the vibration from the engine, I had never felt so much power like that before, I was in awe. Then he said, "When the engine builds up enough air pressure I'll let you sound the horn.

I looked over at him and was very serious when I asked, "Do you think I could go with you next time you leave? He looked at me and knew why I asked him that question and said,"You don't have to be afraid, I'm going to talk to my wife I promise." I smiled and said,"Okay". Then he said,"It's ready". He opened the cab door and stepped down to the first step holding onto the rail. He told me to come over and stand on the driver's seat. Then he pointed to the rope hanging just inside the driver's door and said, "See that rope, grab a hold of it real tight and pull down". With one hand I pulled on the rope and nothing happened. He chuckled telling me I had to pull harder. I reached with both hands this time bending forward and putting my weight into it. The horn was so loud it startled me and my hands let go falling forward out of the cab.

Thanks to his quick reactions he caught me by the back of the shirt as I dangled in the air for a moment then he swung me back towards the cab, then boosted me back up on the seat. He laughed saying, "Careful now, we don't want to lose you. Then he reached over and turned off the engine. He climbed down to the ground and held out his arms telling me to jump. I didn't even hesitate, I trusted him. Safely in his arms he asked me if I was hungry. Of course, I was starving, literally! In all the excitement the thought of food never crossed my mind. Don't ask me why, maybe it was because I was so used to the half and half meal and some days not at all.

He carried me inside the house and upstairs to my room. He set me down and told me he would have his wife make us both something to eat. When he had left, I looked at the toys on the bed and quickly had them on the floor letting my mind run free. For the first time since I'd been there I actually felt secure.

After a while I was so absorbed with the toys, I didn't even hear the man come back upstairs. As he handed me my plate with a sandwich and potato chips, he placed my glass of milk on the nightstand. I looked at him and he smiled as he turned and walked back downstairs. It was a good thing, because I began stuffing my mouth as fast as I could swallow it.

I remember my glands tingling as my mouth began to drool trying to savour every bite. Within minutes my plate and glass of milk were empty. I sat there for a minute or so with my eyes glazed over from the sudden rush of food. My stomach had shrunk from the lack of food and I felt like a beachball on stilts. In a normal situation I could put away twice that much. I sat there on the bed and as the minutes passed I could barely keep my eyes open.

The fear that this woman had instilled in me kept me from lying down on my bed to rest. The lack of sleep and the beating my mind and body had taken, brought me to the point of total exhaustion. As I stood up I almost fell down. My body didn't know how to react to the unexpected consumption of food, it felt like a massive sugar rush. I knew I had to sleep, because my eyes and legs couldn't hold their own weight. I thought if I just shut the door I could lie down on the bed; but it wouldn't be locked like before and there wouldn't be enough time to get off the bed and I couldn't risk that.

Besides, the warm air coming from downstairs was too comforting. So I staggered towards the comer by the payned windows and squatted down and went out like a light. I was only asleep for what seemed like moments; I was still hungry. My body was requiring more nourishment.

Attempting to stand, I had forgotten about the last time I went to my feet and the dizziness caught me off guard once again. I braced myself against the window trying to keep from falling down as my body tingled and my eyes were blinded by the massive head rush. It was only a matter of seconds, but my eyes soon cleared and my balance returned. Feeling confident, I walked towards the door and I was about to call out to he man when I was stopped by the slightly elevated conversation coining from downstairs. I couldn't hear very well so I ventured ever so slowly into the hallway standing against the wall near the railing. The whole conversation from what I could make out boiled down to the fact that neither one of them really wanted me there.

My heart sank as I listened to their heartless words. The hopelessness that I felt in the closet returned, making me feel worthless and empty inside. I couldn't believe it, I trusted him!

Quickly and as silently as possible, I rushed back to my room and stood in the corner and stared at the toys on the floor. Suddenly the toys brought no interest to me anymore, Ya think! I was beginning to think the only reason he was being nice to me was to save his own hide in case anything did happen to me. My curiosity got the best of me and I had to hear more. Walking over to the hallway, I crept towards the wall and peered through the railing as I caught a glimpse of the man coming from the kitchen with her right behind him still arguing. I remained close to the door trying to hear more but they had gone down the hallway into the den and I could only hear mumbling. I stood there thinking to myself, "I have to get out of here, but I didn't have any idea where I was, or where I would go, but I felt I would be doing them both a favor if I just left. But how? I looked downstairs at the front door and the wheels began to turn.

Now this is the part I want everyone to understand, young and old. Here was a three year child determined to leave a somewhat safe environment and venture into the woods twenty miles from any civilization that he knew of. This is what happens to many children with their lives full of mental, physical and sexual abuse. That's why there are so many runaway teens nowadays, and many adults like to believe that the children bring it all upon themselves.

A certain percentage do, but the rest is pure neglect! This is why God had me write this book filled with darkness and despair, but also showing his grace and merciful love through Jesus Christ.

I waited for the right time when they were both busy, and I silently crept downstairs. I could hear her in the kitchen and he was in the den watching television. I figured since they had been arguing that the chances of them coming from either direction was slim and none. I stood in front of the door and looked up at the lock that seemed endlessly out of reach. But don't ask me why, but there was a chair right next to the door. The entryway had wood floors so this was going to be difficult, but no different than at home when I used to slide the chair across the linoleum floor so I could get into the refrigerator without my mother hearing me. As I slowly slid the chair the distance seemed endless, but my determination pushed me to continue, no matter what the outcome may be. Finally with the chair close enough, I cautiously stood and began to turn the lock. Hearing it click, I looked towards the kitchen to see if the woman had heard it. With my heart pounding, I climbed down and moved the chair just enough so I could open the door. I reached up and grabbed the door knob with both hands and turned it to the right and pulled back, it wouldn't budge. I tried again! What was happening, it should open! Then I looked up and above the lock was another one that I hadn't noticed before. This lock demanded a key. My heart sank as I stared at the only obstacle that stood in my way from escaping. But my heart abruptly jumped to my throat when the woman walked out of the kitchen and sternly asked me what I was doing downstairs.

I quickly answered her telling her that I was still hungry. She told me that I would eat when it was time and not anytime sooner. She took me by the hand and briskly led me back to my room. Standing there alone I finally had to accept the fact that I was here to stay and there was nothing I could do or say that would change my situation.

Well my wounds were healing faster as I was eating regularly, and I couldn't really complain because I now had toys to play with and my room wasn't freezing because the door was being left open. Also, for two days I hadn't seen the woman because her husband was bringing me all my meals and putting me to bed at night. I think this man knew something was wrong, because I had been extremely distant since the arguing two days earlier, especially when he asked me if I wanted to see his truck again and I refused. I was really disappointed in his phoney concern. I genuinely thought he cared about me but, hearing their conversation made me worry what would happen when he leaves again.

That night after dinner, the man came and got my dishes, he told me he would be up later to tuck me in. I didn't respond, I just looked at him and he could tell I felt uneasy. Because that morning he told her that he would be leaving tomorrow for another two weeks and I had a bad feeling about that. The man was only downstairs for a short time when I heard the woman screaming at him. From what I could put together, he was confronting her about the abuse she had inflicted upon me, and she was basically calling me a liar. He went on to say, "I saw the welts all over his body, he didn't deserve that, nobody does"! Then she said," You're taking his word over mine, how dare you! It was about that time I heard her screaming and crying as I could hear him slap her several times, telling her to never do that to me again! When I heard this, I actually cheered him on and felt satisfaction hearing him beat her. I know that sounds sick, but my suffering warranted some kind of vengeance since I wasn't big enough to fulfill that obligation.

After the arguing ceased, I felt all would be well now that he had put his foot down and told her that this was to never happen again. I waited patiently for him to come upstairs and tuck me in. I already had my pajamas on as I felt it was about that time. I heard him coming upstairs. He walked into the room and I was attempting to pull back the covers and he leaned. down and helped me finish drawing them back. I jumped into bed not saying a word. Even though I knew he didn't want me there, still I was nice to him as he could see the satisfied look on my face.

As he turned off the light and closed the door part way, I felt some peace as I drifted into a restful slumber. The next morning I woke to the rumbling of the mans roaring diesel that made the windows vibrate. Still half asleep, I sat up in bed rubbing my eyes. I looked and noticed my door was shut and it was freezing in my room. I quickly put on my daily clothing and my jacket, then proceeded to make my bed. Then I heard him reve his engines and begin to back out of the driveway blowing his airhom. This made me jump and also gave me a very sick feeling in my stomach. Then I heard her heavy feet coming upstairs. She opened the door without even looking at me and picked up all the toys and started walking out with them. I told her she couldn't do that, the man gave those to me. She kept going and closed the door. I sat there listening to her mumble to herself as she went back downstairs. Then my hair stood on end and every nerve came alive with fear. She was screaming obscenities, she sounded insane! I jumped from the bed frightened out of my mind when I heard her say, "I'll show you you little bastard"! I ran to the comer and began undressing with vigor hoping she might go easy on me if I already prepared myself. She entered the room with the door slamming against the wall as it bounced back towards her as she pushed it out of the way with a look on her face you could only describe as insane!

She screamed at me saying, "You made my husband hate me you little bastard"! I had just begun to remove my clothes but that didn't matter, the belt began to fly. She wasn't even going to remove my clothes, well not at first. With the belt hitting me from all directions, the next thing I knew she was ripping my clothes off, literally. I was begging her not to do this as she undid my pants. Reaching down to my feet she grabbed both pant legs and upended me slamming my head to the hard tile floor. I was completely naked now as she went crazy. I tried to cover my face and privates, but the belt was covering every inch of my body with full length blows. I screamed rolling every which way trying to avoid her lashes. She then stood me up grabbing me by both wrists in one hand and held them above my head. My mind went into hysteria because I knew what was coming. She let go with full force catching me across the privates. They had barely healed from the last ordeal. The pain was so excruciating I thought I was begining to black out, as I couldnt hear anything, just ringing in my ears as I watched the silent blows torture my manhood. It was like watching a silent horror movie in slow motion. She let go of my arms as I fell to the floor, but it wasn't over yet. she reached down grabbing me by the hair and began dragging me across the tile floor. I slid easily for a moment and it wasn't bad because the floor was so cold, and to be truthful, my body was in shock so I really didn't feel the rug cut at my wounds as he dragged me towards the closet. She stood me up and shoved me in the closet locking the door behind me.

My body was numb and in total darkness except for the light coming from under the door, I remained standing, feeling nothing and in complete silence. It was a few minutes before my hearing returned, and with it immense pain. I thought I was hurt before, but nothing compared to the welts this time. Even my privates were bleeding, I could feel the blood running down the inside of my legs. My body began to shake uncontrollably from the immense heat coming from my wounds and the cool air in the closet. My gut feeling was telling me that I was going to die right here in this closet. Well from past experience I knew I had to lie down before my welts had a chance to heal. Squatting down, my buttocks gently touched the floor adding more pressure as I began to sit. Then I jumped up dancing like my skin was on fire. I felt like I had been doused in gasoline and set to blaze. My bare feet sensed something foreign on the floor. I bent over and swept my hand across the floor. It felt like sand, it wasn't, it was salt again! I was smarter this time. I quickly brushed the salt to one side of the closet so I could lie down.

Well, I can't say time flew by, because it didn't. As I had mentioned when I first got into the closet I knew I was going to die in here, I was correct. It was four days I had been in here according to the rise and fall of the sun. I could feel I was losing weight, my arms felt like skin and bones. My body had expelled all that it was going to and I had passed the stage of hunger. I was so weak I didn't even have the energy to cry anymore. I wasn't sleeping at all during the day; well barely. All I was doing was staring at the light coming from under the door in a hypnotic state. I couldn't even muster up enough brain waves to play with my imaginary friends. Of course at night I would have to wait for the rat to return which wasn't until early morning and even then it was hard to fall asleep because the smell of breakfast would antagonize my empty stomach.

The days dragged on endlessly. I woke one morning after I had gone to sleep to the phone ringing outside my door and I heard her answer the phone downstairs. I pulled myself towards the gap under the door and listened to the conversation. I was hoping it was her husband, and maybe if I screamed loud enough he would hear me, but it wasn't. Instead it was my case worker. I could hear the woman telling her how sick I was and that I couldn't come to the phone. I knew I had to do something. I mustered up all my reserve energy kicking at the door wildly and screaming as loud as I could! It paid off, because I heard her coming upstairs.

He opened the door and told me my worker wanted to talk to me. Leaning down she warned me that if I told her what she was doing to me she would kill me before she got here, her look told me she was serious. I nodded to her that I wouldn't. I stood up and she picked up the phone outside the closet, she handed it to me as the case worker asked me how I was doing. I looked at the woman and I couldn't answer, all I could do was start crying. I tried to say something, anything, but I was babbling so bad she couldn't understand me. She tried to comfort me by expressing that she understood I was sick and that I would get better. I stopped crying for a moment. I could barely get the words out that I wished she could come and see me, but she said she had so many children to take care of that she didn't have the time; besides it was tO\lfar for her to come all the way out there. I looked at the woman trying to decide whether or not to say something, but I saw the look in the woman's eyes and I knew she would carry out her threat. I began to start crying again, my worker said she wanted to talk to the woman so I handed her the phone. I stood there as the woman lied to her telling her how sick I was. She said her goodbyes and hung up the phone. She then turned me around and escorted me back into the closet and locked the door.

Two days had passed by and still no food, and I knew I was dying. I began looking back on how I had treated my brother and I felt so ashamed for what I had done. I thought back about the kids in the neighborhood and how they talked about God. They said you can't see him but he's there, all you have to do is talk to him and he'll be there for you. Well I had nothing to lose, so I began to talk to God. The first time I asked him If he could make me bigger so I could knock down the door and kill this woman, I waited but nothing happened. So I layed there another day in a pathetic state of hopelessness. I didn't move at all, even when the rat came out I was t()))weak to be scared. That morning I decided to try and talk to God once more asking for forgiveness for what I had done. I said, "God, if you get me out of this closet and out of this house, I will never do what I did to my brother or anyone else ever again.

Suddenly, I felt a presence and a warmth enveloping all around me and my stomach felt like it was being filled, not with food, but with love. I sat up not knowing what to think of my renewed strength. A few minutes later the phone rang. The woman answered it right outside the door, she had already been upstairs. I listened, it was my worker again. She then opened the door holding the phone to her chest telling me it was my case worker and that she wanted to talk to me.

Once again she reminded me, "If you say anything to her about what I've done, I will make sure you're dead before she gets here and she'll never find you". She handed me the phone. I tried talking to her but all I could do was cry. The woman had me so scared I couldn't even talk. My worker said she couldn't understand me and that she wanted to talk to the woman. I handed her the phone crying and stomping my feet in frustration.

The woman said, "Excuse me for a moment", covering the phone, she told me that she was going downstairs and if I picked up the phone she would kill me. Now this was the third time she had threatened my life. She went downstairs as I listened to her conversation expressing again how sick I was. I could tell she was getting ready to hang up and it was now or never. I knew if I didn't, I surely was going to die! Both apprehensive and terrified, I courageously picked up the phone and started screaming for her to come and get me. She asked me what she had been doing to me and I couldn't answer knowing she was on the other line. I sat there in silence petrified to say anything.

My worker sensed there was something wrong and told me to hang up because she wanted to talk to the woman. I set down the phone as I stood there naked and helpless and smelling of a dung heap. I heard her hang up the phone, then she came upstairs. She stood there looking at me and said, "She's coming to see. you". She led me by the hand towards the bathroom. I stood there as she drew my bathwater. When it was full, she picked me up and set me in the tub which was so hot I started screaming and flailing around as my privates felt like they were going to burn off. She took me out and ran some cold water in the tub until it was suitable for bathing. I couldn't believe she did that but I was relieved.

In the tub she had no mercy as she scrubbed my welts trying to remove the remaining scabs. It hurt so bad but she didn't care. All she could do was scream at me to stop crying. She kept reminding me what would happen if I told my worker what she'd done. She told me that when my worker was done with her visit, I would be punished for disobeying her by getting on the phone.

After she had dressed me, she brought the toys back in the room that she had taken away trying to make it look like a happy home.

When my worker had shown up she brought her upstairs. The woman walked in first and gave me a look that didn't need words. My worker walked in behind her and the first words that came out of her mouth was, "My you have been sick, you're skin and bones". She looked at the woman and asked her if I had been seen by a doctor. The woman replied, "I called the doctor and he said it was probably the flu since he couldn't hold any food down. He told me to keep him in bed and give him plenty of fluids. The woman acted so nice I couldn't believe it was the same person.

I started crying and my worker looked at me and took my hand saying, "Come on John lets go downstairs it's kind of chilly in here. We stood in front of the door and my worker opened it and told me to go wait in the car, she needed to talk to the woman and that she would be out in a few minutes to get me. I stood there for a moment as she shut the door. I felt paralyzed. What should I do? Should I run, I could hide in the woods and they wouldn't even find me, or I could hide in the backseat and maybe she wouldn't see me and drive off taking me with her. I decided to go to the car and hide.

I opened the door and closed it behind me and layed down on the floor. In a little while she came out to the car and looked in the front seat but I wasn't there. She looked in the back window and saw me on the floor. She opened the door and told me I needed to go back inside with her because she had to leave. I started crying so hard I was choking and I don't believe I even had enough fluids in me to draw a tear. She looked at me and knew something wasn't right. "Okay John, stay here and I'll be right back.

When she came back she sat up front and told me to come up there because she wanted to talk to me. I crawled over to the seat and layed on the floor looking up at her with distrust and fear in my eyes. Quietly and gently she asked me if she had been beating me. I didn't say anything, I just stared at her remembering what the woman had said. She said, "It's okay John you can tell me, has she been beating you? In response I shook my head yes. She told me to come and sit by her. I got up on the seat. She told me to remove my shirt. As I took off my shirt she saw the welts that were criss crossed all over me. I told her that she had washed the scabs off and that they looked worse before. She told me that she could see them clearly. Then she asked me to remove my pants and I asked her if she was going to beat me too. She said, "No, I just want to take a look".

It was hard pulling down my pants sitting down as they dragged across my privates. So I stood on the floor and when I pulled them all the way down she gasped sitting back as she saw my privates that were still scabbed. She turned me around and saw the many lashes I had on my backside. She started crying saying, "John, I am so sorry, I want you to know I had no idea she was doing this to you".

I started to cry as she helped me to get dressed being very gentle as she pulled up my pants. She told me to wait there and that she would be right back.

I sat there not knowing if she was just going to talk to her, or was I going to be leaving. When she returned, she found me back on the floor. She told me I could come and lay my head on her lap. I climbed up and layed my weary head on her lap. We drove off as she cried with soothing words saying, "Don't worry John, you'll never have to go back there ever again". That was the last thing I remember until I went to the next home.

To this day I fear total darkness, being locked up, I am claustrophobic, I am afraid of rats, I can't go to the bathroom in front of anybody and when I am threatened, I start to nut up. Also, I am hit hard enough, I blackout and feel no pain and my adrenaline is twice that of a normal person, they call it the kindling effect.

I've had to live with this pain and drenching nightmares from

P. T.S.D. For those who don't know what that is, it's post traumatic stress disorder. I am now 48 years old and God and Jesus has helped me to cope with it, but sometimes stress creeps into my life and it brings back the nightmares. I told my psychiatrist that I thought after so many years and treatment that this would all go away, but he told me if I thought that, I was fooling myself. There are many men and women who live with these secrets. Some remember and some keep them tucked neatly away in a locked closet in their minds. I hope this gives other men the courage to put away their false pride and ask God to unlock their secret doors so they can put to rest those fits of anger and rage that surface for no apparent reason, so we think. A Lot of us act out in rage from our past and it has to stop. It can be healed if you ask Jesus to enter your life and his warm embrace will soothe your aching heart.

HAVE WE EVER MET?

I've been searching for you all my life, but I can't seem to find you; it hurts so bad, like a cut from a knife.

I've been so lost for so many years, wandering the streets endlessly, with my eyes full of tears.

It's hard to feel the true meaning of joy until I find you; you're the other half of my soul that will make me whole and complete my earthly goal.

Where are you? Why can't we seem to meet, I wonder sometimes if I've passed you by on the street?

I feel the times when you're so sad, I feel the times when you're happy and glad.

I long to feel your gentle touch or the smooth caress of your dainty little feet; oh, why can't we seem to meet?

I've met so many, but none have ever filled my heart. Oh, why can't we seem to meet? I've loved only you from the very start.

I know why we haven't met; our souls aren't ready yet.

When God knows it's time, the wedding bells will chime, and our hearts will be joined as one in a glorious rhyme...

Joy to us, who have waited so long,
To learn God's word and how to be strong.
To fight Satan, when he does us wrong,
To cling together in an endless bond.

Though he may try to pull us apart,
by throwing the past in our faces, we know
how to do battle, because now we hold all the aces.

LIFE

Jesus says, "Love thy neighbor as thyself, relinquish your hate, and receive God's wealth."

For no matter how much money we spend or how much we lend, there is nothing that can replace the love that Jesus can send.

His words speak of wisdom, truth, and love; behold his power and strength that come from the heavens above.

Look to the sky as you live each day and remember his words, which you will hear when you pray.

Life can be meaningless or it can be a blessing for those you meet if you just remember to be humble as you lay before Jesus at his feet.

THEY TOUCH ME

Today, I saw a moving sight, two people caught in the delight of the Lord.

Their shining voices brought tears to my eyes and lifted my spirit as they said their goodbyes.

It was God who I saw, shining in their eyes, a sparkle that glistened as others cried.

It was tears of joy that everyone felt, a moving experience that made my uneasiness melt.

God has touched them, you see, to show His sparkling spirit and miraculous deeds.

His message was strong and a lasting light, that sends my heart reeling on an endless flight.

GOING HOME

Going home seems to be tough at times, as we fear the outcome of what we might leave behind.

Those things that seemed so precious to us, our friends, our families, the people we've touched, oh, those things we'll miss so much.

Our memories are filled with thoughts from the beginning to the end, and sometimes we wish that God would let us do it again.

There comes a time when we should remember the deeds we've done, the many we've met, and there was so much fun.

There was laughter, there was pain, there was truly joy, because God was there in every little girl and boy.

Remember, only the heart of a child will enter the Kingdom of Heaven and no other; this we must share with all our Sisters and Brothers.

For the words of the Lord should fill our minds with the truth of His promise at the end of the line.

So keep your thoughts in a steady stream, for if you don't, it's just a wish and nothing but a dream; so remember the land of milk and honey and the sweet thoughts of peaches and cream.

I dedicate this poem to a close friend of mine, for whom I was proud to have known, even though it was short; the memories live on of Donald John Ritola.

THROUGH MY EYES

Every day that passes by, I consume more of God's words, and I pass them on through my eyes!

People hear His words, they see my eyes, they wonder how and they wonder why.

I can't explain this holy bliss, but I can show others what they've missed.

God's words work through my heart, they surface everywhere, even in my art.

I remember when I talked with my head, and people saw in my eyes that my heart was dead.

But now when I speak, God touches many, so many who are weak.

They're weak in various ways or sin, weak in their hearts, for their old ways remain as they refuse to refrain and still cling to their haunting pain.

If they knew me from before and knew what I've done, it would be so clear the change I've made. Then their eyes would be open to God's purpose and accept His precious Son.

THE SHADOW OF THE CROSS

Let the spirit of the cross reach out to those in the land, telling the people that this is God's healing hand.

He's reaching to you, and His love runs deep. He grieves for those who don't believe, and His heart is sad so, quietly alone He weeps.

He wants everyone to know of His Son's return, to read His words and pass on what we've learned.

For there will be a time for all to see, the shadow of the cross, meant just for you and me.

They enrich our lives, this Holy Trinity, giving us peaceful thoughts with love and serenity.

The shadow of the cross spreads throughout the land, covering a multitude of acreage, its beam stretching across an endless span.

The shadow rests as the sun slowly fades away, only to return once more, for another day.

A Different Light

As we grew from childhood, everything seemed so cheerful and bright. We found things to be so simple and free. Then, why couldn't our parents just leave us alone and let us be?

We thought to ourselves, "We can do this on our own." But as we fell flat on our faces, people were there to tell us that we were not alone.

Until we decide to let love into our hearts, life has no meaning, and there is no real start.

Beginning with our soul, this is what keeps us alive: the yearning for knowledge and the strength to make great strides.

The light we emit is so cheerful and gay, it could turn a sky blue that once was gray.

If we could harness this invisible light, we could teach others who grovel from fear and fright.

Life was simple at one time, but many decided to go against God, and that was a crime.

Down through the ages, we've paid for our sins, with Jesus' blood, and sometimes our kin.

So battle if you may, and lose if you might, but never lose track of the ways of the light.

FRIENDSHIP IS GENUINE

The first sight of your sparkling eyes, I felt freedom coming from your comfortable smile.

Your eyes shone like a neon light, making me feel so open and free.

You remind me of the feeling I get when the sun must rest and the day must end; the cresting moon brings on the night, and the evening is set. I have to tell you, you bring out my very best.

For I have found a friend who could open my heart; I felt so free that I can say anything to you from the very start.

I don't know what will happen as the days go on; all I can do is express how I feel: that my friendship is genuine, and my respect for you is real.

THEY SHINE LIKE THEIR SHOES

Are they for real or not? Does it really matter? Just look how they shine while making all that clatter!

Does it truly hurt to try something new and join the others who sit in the pews, the people who shine like their shoes?

They seems real, a likable bunch; not some crazy fanatics who are out to lunch.

They're happy and free from their worldly sins. With God's grace, they never have to live in Satan's world again!

WHEN THE LIGHT COMES ON

When the light comes on and the moon is full, I see you, God; you're so wonderful. There's a feeling I get for my past regrets… I don't deserve you now.

Let me serve you now and lift me up, so my eyes may see the light. To the truth be known, filled with delight… how wonderful you are.

Help me, God. Teach me how to be a friend to all concerned. Show me love, to love discerned… how wonderful you are.

I'm your child now. I show no fear because I know you now, and I know you're near. I know your love, and I'll hold it so dear, how wonderful you are.

Within the light, there's so much love. You can believe me now that God is above. So show him now, to let him see you're what he wants you to be.

GOD IS THE CURE

There's a time for living and a time for play, a time with God that's pleasing to say.

I'm alone with God, in silence resting in my cot. I used to feel alone, but now I'm not.

My life has changed; it's slow but sure, and God leads my life for He is the cure.

The cure begins when we profess and give God's true words away, to others who are unsure how to go about their day.

I'm striving towards the day when I will become pure, as long as I read God's words, I will have the strength to endure.

Letting people see God's wonderful works, to walk in His path without our strange little quirks.

It's a belief all its own and a heartfelt way, it's joy, it's peace, it's freedom today.

Just a word, a smile, a simple touch, is that too hard, or asking too much?

There are some who walk the ways of the Lord, but in their actions, their thoughts are so loud. I can see them hover over their heads, like a dark grey cloud.

Sometimes I wish I didn't have this gift of sight, that's why so many times I've fled in fright, because I tell the truth, and they don't want to admit that I'm right.

No matter how far I ran, or where I go, Satan is always there, trying to ruin the show.

His actions show in people who aren't steadfast in their belief. I know I am now, and that's such relief. Harnessing God's awesome power within our hearts, it's a picture we paint, that's the knowledge of art.

As long as I continue to let God show me the way, I will grow stronger and stronger with every passing day.

My Strength is God's Guidance

Your guidance and love are two things I hear each day, the things you whisper to me as I pray.

This gives me strength, and I don't just walk the line; I spread your words like a wondrous feast, that you invite others to dine.

You guide me to people who hunger for your words, and then you reward me with the sight of your beautiful birds.

Your spirit is vibrant inside my soul; you teach through me and show others how to be free and whole.

My eyes sparkle with your presence inside; they see the change and how you helped me when I cried.

Glory be to you, Lord God, the one and only King. You bring what they seek, your heavenly words, oh how the truth does ring.

They want to become your servants, to be weak in your watchful eyes. All they want is to be heard, Lord God, as they kneel before you and cry.

I FEAR ONLY ONE

My fears used to run so deep inside, the open scars I just couldn't hide.

What's different about me today, you say? I can stop someone and say, "Hello, hey, I love you, bro'. Would you care to have lunch someday?"

It had to do with being honest with God, to tell Him I was weak, so afraid for my life, and of the terrible mistakes I've made.

To really reach down deep inside, to find those feelings I've been trying to hide.

The anger, the frustration, the fear, the mistrust, the hopelessness in the search for someone to trust.

I found the trust I needed when I let Jesus control my thoughts, to have Him release my pain when my stomach was tied in knots.

Jesus is the key, you see, because there's only one I fear and many who seek, His spirit who knows our every thought and brings out our tears of joy while we imagine Him holding us tight, as He kisses us like a child on the cheek.

HUMILITY: TO BE OR NOT TO BE

I led my life thinking I was better than everyone else, so I feared all things and kept my pride hidden on the shelf.

The truth was, I was afraid to be me. If I showed the real me, people would say I was being weak, and I was told that wasn't the manly way.

Looking back on the lies I told myself, I see with perfect vision how lost I was, begging for the time God would set me free.

Sometimes it's embarrassing and humorous how I used to isolate myself from those around me. But now I see I sold myself short, being both special and unworthy.

It was frightening not knowing which way to turn, for my pride held me bound and told me, "Stand tall, stand proud, stand your ground, expound your rage out loud."

Well, that was a lie, and I found out why when I dropped my pride and asked God to help me sigh.

There was a peace instilled in me, and God showed me all about love and true serenity.

I became that moldy old clay that God began to shape as I continued to believe and pray.

He said one day, as I kneeled to pray, "My child, I have a task for you, and you'll perform it well. Just let me mold your soul, for you will have lots to tell."

Well, I cried with joy that God had chosen this sinful, angry boy!

I now had purpose and a direction I could turn, for now I had a reason and a willingness to learn. Reading Scriptures and praying with friends kept me from defiance and feelings of defense.

Jesus is my inspiration, and He inspires my mind, that I can now express in words to others what He'll do for you if you just give Him time!

When we become more open and let God search our hearts, we'll feel His love more and more as He removes the evil parts.

As the days go on, the Spirit of God may come to you as a singing bird on a branch or a spontaneous hello from a small child as they giggle and dance.

The Spirit of God is there every day, but our eyes need to be open to see His glorious ways.

If our eyes aren't on the glory of God, we will interpret our own truth, and our minds will become cluttered and filled with sod.

William Shakespeare once said, "All the world's a stage, and the people in it are mere players of a role. If we decide to live in God's world, we must be ready to face Jesus at every turn and feel that we are unworthy of His grace. For He wants us to play a role as children who are willing to learn, showing true feelings of humility and none of disgrace."

STEPPING AWAY FROM THE SADDLE

What are feelings? Can they be touched or discarded and thrown away, like an obstacle that has struck a nerve and gotten in your way?

Knowing and not caring, you lash out with feelings of pain. You hurt others as you let go of the reins.

Feeling the wild horse run free, it steps on anything in its way. This is expected from someone who has lost themselves and been led astray.

Flailing their arms in a desperate travail, the wild stallion takes them for a ride on an endless lonely trail.

His nostrils flare with sweat dripping from his side, his tireless legs will take you for one thoughtless ride.

He flies like the wind at the speed of light, giving you nothing but a battered body and a ghastly flight.

As the stallion takes its toll on your body and your spirit is broken, you think to yourself, "Can I jump from this stallion? What will people say or be spoken?"

Unless a person is willing to take that chance, to fly from the stallion's back, to tumble and fall, they'll never know what it's like to be humble before God and hear His words at all. Of course, once again we think to ourselves, "What will happen? What will people think if they see me break my prideful shell?"

Well, what does it take for you to drop your pride and admit to God that you're weak and you feel empty inside?

Not convinced yet? You may want to reconsider the saddle and remember the time before. Who's to say what will happen again or what's really in store?

Can you really take that chance and ride the wild stallion again, to see once more who will win? Or will you let God be your guide and show you what it's like to have Jesus within?

THE LONE SPIRIT

The lone spirit rides the plains, searching for his people who wander, stripped of their pride, looking for their feelings that are no longer inside.

He's beside himself, with no one to ease his pain, his soul is barren, taken from the people caught in self-gain.

Please, God, forgive his darkened heart, for he knows not of the evil one in this world. It's now eating at his love and into a spin he is hurled.

This evil favors only suffering and tragedy, telling lies to those whose hearts are empty and bleeding.

The lone spirit keeps riding the plains, hoping to find the truth to his troubled pain. The truth is the word of God. By His grace, may the lone spirit be open to accepting His son Jesus Christ and seeking His face, feeling His warm caress and loving embrace.

SAVING AMMUNITION

Since I've been walking with the Lord, I've tried to do what He asks in His ways and in His words. No more can I do those things that were so sinful and absurd.

I offer my hand, asking for nothing in return. I ask for forgiveness, for this is new for me to learn.

I used to be stern when I wanted a favor returned, as I would ask someone, and they would look me straight in the eye, it would be followed by a frown and, "Sorry, I've got something to do, I don't recall ever saying I'd help you!"

I would look at them without saying a word, and in my mind, I would say, "I'll show you. I have plenty of time, I'll get even someday!"

I'm like an elephant, I never forget. One day when you need a hand, I'll say I'll be there, but you just remember when you left me hanging, feeling like no one cared.

You see, you shouldn't do that to someone who's been saving those secrets that you tell, because they'll surface in the mix of the crowd, and in their minds, they'll ponder and dwell.

I used to save a barrage of information, stored for my own personal use, but now I save, and I don't share, so I don't have to make any excuse.

It's personal and told in confidence, no one else needs to know; it's not for the time when you are bored and blind or idle conversation for show.

It's a trust that was given to you and no other because they let down their walls and treated you like a sister or brother. Now there's another kind of ammunition I used to save, the ones who hurt my feelings that set my mind ablaze.

I've offered my hand in so many ways, but if someone turns you down even when you're just trying to help, they refuse you the right to do God's work; I don't know about you, but this would bring out my old ways, and into my head Iwould lurk.

Oh, I know what it is, the old pride thing, that old ball and chain; "I can do this all on my own," that heavy weight that keeps us locked in Satan's evil reign, that's so selfish, so insane!

So when someone offers you a hand or does something nice on demand, be careful, be thoughtful, be kind, and remember these words I tell: "Be thankful and be glad that person was there, because if you don't, in the future, you may need them, and they won't be there."

That's why God says, "Love thy neighbor as thyself, put away self-gain and pride because if you don't learn now, it will follow you to hell; like the sow and her hide that wallowed in her mess just moments before she died!"

GOD TEACH ME HOW TO PRAY

Oh, heavenly Father, teach me how to pray. Fill my heart, fill my mind, and teach me what to say.

I read Your words and profess Your name. Teach me now as I proclaim Your fame.

Your wondrous works are full of praises. I read and I read, but I remember very few phrases.

There is one that speaks to me loud and clear, and these words we should speak, even to those who are unwilling to hear:

"Once someone has escaped the corruption of the world, by knowing our lord and savior, Christ Jesus and are again entangled in it and overcome, it would be better for them to have never known me at all."
~2 peter 2:20

I think that really sums it up: to know I'm still a baby, just a young little pup.

But I still feel like I'm not doing enough. I feel useless, like a diamond in the rough.

Please, Father, teach me how to pray. If it's Your will, I shall remain steadfast and still.

I know Your plan, yet I can't remember Your words. I know Your love; so much of this I've heard.

Is it selfish to ask for more? I don't know. I need You now while on my knees on the floor.

Show me, Father, teach me more. I'm hungry, I'm thirsty, feed me, I implore.

I may not use Scriptures fluently from my mouth, but my head and my heart carry two strong hands, a royal flush, and a full house.

I may be poor, but my heart is rich. You know my scars, for they still remain to be stitched.

I have received Your message; it's loud and clear. I see Your plan for those who ingest Your words and the plans for those who practice idolatry and jeer.

BACK FROM THE PAST

Listen to the story of a man lost inside, one which has made it and lost it according to his pride.

There's a lesson to be learned from my wayward ways, a welcome challenge to return from the burning haze.

I've seen it, I've done it, and I'm not proud of my ways, but now I've returned and I'm counting the days.

Freedom from death is a reward all its own, to know the right path and ask to be shown.

I believe this now, and I really want to learn how to become who I am without any worries or discerns.

My past is my past, but those days sometimes return. This is the time to sacrifice the flesh, for Satan would love to see me get burned.

Returning from the past isn't any simple task, just remember to remain loyal and true, as God will give you anything that you ask while helping you down the path that you ensue.

YOU'VE TOUCH ME

I asked you from afar, and yet you're so near, when you hear my cries for help and lend me your ear.

You've waited so long to hear my voice, to grip my life and make a choice.

You helped me break my chains and step into a world of love, to see the hate I held inside, to see the barrier that was only pride.

Oh God, how I've longed to feel your presence and reach out to your loving hands. I remember the poem that touched my heart when you carried that man in the sand.

Now that I see the real me inside and left the other behind, I'm asking you, God, to help show me the way and learn how to be helpful and kind.

FILLING MY HEART

I always put one foot in front of the other as I climb through the dense brush, absorbing everything that I see. I take my time on my uphill climb because I know there's no need to rush.

I let the scent and sounds fill my senses to capacity. This helps remind me of the simplicity of my life, that I am who I am, and for my Father, I'll bear many sufferings and strife.

I fill my heart with all that I see, asking God to instill the truth and who He wants me to be.

The peacefulness of God's own world makes my heart beat strong, while filling empty voids with peaceful thoughts, making me see that nothing can go wrong.

As I go deeper and higher into what life has to offer, my sight is in awe of the beauty of the illustrious trees. They grow to be giants, and this brings me to my knees.

I pray to my Father, for which I can feel, thanking Him with a joyful cheer. As I look to the heavens and shout out loud, I tell God I'm ready for His words and for knowing Him, I'm proud.

Still gazing up above, I see powder blue skies. This brings me joy and tears to my eyes.

Without God in my life, I would not be alive to glimpse once more at the glorious sky just over the rise.

Oh, how I've longed to feel this way, to truly feel His presence when I pray.

The longing for laughter, which mends my heart, I reach to those who have come to their end and are looking for a brand-new start.

I know these feelings will last forever as long as I have God in my life. I know this to be true; I can feel it, can't you?

My heart is full of love and hope for all mankind, praying for forgiveness and not being so blind.

    I can start for a change by filling my heart with faith, secure and calm. God mends my life, making me bold and strong. The love in my heart will beat everlasting and strong.

WE

We are not alone, and we can be free once more, to shed our hardened hides and become who we were before.

I know it's rough, and times may seem tough living on our hopes and our dreams. Our wayward ways made us depend on ourselves, as we feared the many, and it seemed too lonely and scary to tell.

If we run on self-will and not on "we," we will forget about the others. This would send us back on blindfolded sprees.

This spree is a wild place of sinful lust and dismal disgrace, a venture that can lead us astray.

The longer we wait, the more sick we become, and we hide more feelings as we run and run.

It's a vicious cycle that has to stop, a bubble we're blowing that's about to pop.

Can we stop? Can we be free? The only ones who can change are you and me.

There is a combination that completes as one, to be with God, there's much more hope, feelings, and fun.

So the cycle can be broken, and we can heal those open sores. All we have to remember is: God is there, and (we) can stop and say, "No more!"

JUST A WOODEN WHEEL

Cool, crisp waters flow around a wooden wheel. This touches my heart because I'm alive, and I know how to feel.

It's not just being alive; it's the hope and care I can see in other people's eyes.

When we're down and alone, we think of the easy way out. We look to the sky and begin to shout of the pain, the fears, and the doubt.

There's always a struggle to find our true selves. We're not neatly hidden or placed high on a shelf. We just want to know God and get out of ourselves.

When we're alone in nature's wonders, we should let our minds absorb and feast on every color that we see. This will soften our wooden hearts and remove bad feelings, those godly feelings that kept us apart.

It allows kindness and love to flow through our veins, for we know not who we are, but we do know the pain.

There are some that believe what they see and not what they feel because all they can see is but a wet wooden wheel.

THE STAMP

Some people don't understand when God lends a hand; His moves are so fast, like the sleight of hand.

We think it's just luck when we find a buck, but just moments before, we were down on our luck.

It happens again and again, but we just can't see, it's God's anonymous hands that He shows to you and me.

God says, "Knock and the door shall open."

He's proven to me so many times that He's listening intently, like some finely tuned chimes.

I once said to God, "Let me find a nickel for a stamp that I need," and God said, "I know what you want" and let me intercede.

Well, I was short on funds, and I walked towards the door, and there, at my feet, was a stamp on the floor.

Now, just moments before, when I had walked through the door, the floor was bare, and there was nothing for me to score.

You see, God gave me what I needed and not what I want. It's so simple, just ask, and His hands will do even that small little task.

FATHER, I NEED A HUG

Going to my knees, I pray to my Father for a gentle little squeeze.

It's not much that I ask, it's a favor my heart does need, a simple hug, a gentle touch. This I pray, this I plead.

Father, it's so hard for me to hug myself because my old ways seem to find their way down from the shelf.

I've put them so high up out of my reach, but somehow they tend to fall back into my speech.

I am human, and I do make mistakes, so help me, Lord, and hold me tight. Let me feel your love and your words of might.

I've read your words, I embrace your love. Now let me expound your grace and tell of your deeds, as I hold my hands and praise your name and confess how you always meet my needs.

LOVE THY NEIGHBOR

Once we're in the light of Christ, we know what is wrong, and we know what is right.

There are some who will say that they've accepted His ways, but in their speech, they will show they still stray.

Now, it's hard to love someone who still plays those games, the ones who have yet to stop Satan's evil reign.

We listen to their words, we bite our tongues. We have to remember, we were there once, and our minds are still young.

It seems impossible to love our neighbor when they insult us so, but we need only pray for them, for they know not the things we know.

Sure, we could lash out in our old sinful ways, but God helps us to remember this simple little phrase: "It is mine to avenge; I will repay," says the Lord. On the contrary, "if your enemy is hungry, feed him; if he is thirsty, give him drink."

In doing this, you will heap burning coals upon his head…

That phrase has helped me to learn that now it's time to let God have His turn.

He sees the people who walk the line, the ones who laugh and just do their time.

The night is nearly over; the day is almost here. So let us put aside the deeds of darkness and put on the armor of light, so we don't have to fear.

God will protect you in all that you do. Just let Him do His job, so you don't have to stress like you used to do.

DIVINE SERENITY

Calmness in the air and a mirror reflection are mere images for anyone to see. As for those who have lost their way, can only hear the pebble plunge, making the crisp scenery form ripples and sway.

For those that are not careful, can slip into the pond, they will lose sight from the distortion and from the days beyond.

We see the birds, so carefree in flight, moving about like rustling leaves. It's nature's way of saying, "We must stay in our hearts and never leave".

It's hard to be humble and even tougher to be weak, but this is God's strength, and He shows us we can be meek.

Letting our minds absorb what God has shown us so far, we can make a new beginning because we are who we are.

What we've learned can be a role for others to follow, because our lives are full, not all empty and hollow.

We must make the ripples subside and have the reflection returned. Then, we can be humble for everyone to see, this shows them the beauty of life and divine serenity.

POETRY

Poetry is music, its moments are true.

Poetry has many meanings; it can be heartwarming or blue.

The perception is different, no matter how

you perceive the thought, it's always true.

There's a feeling you'll get, and it's meant just for you.

Look at its structure, feel its disguise, and the picture

will appear right in front of your eyes.

Feel the tingle, feel the stir, and the sigh of relief,

what poetry will bring, while also taking away your grief.

INNER PEACE

Sometimes we hem and haw for the truth, and it always seems to get stuck in our craw.

It's hard sometimes to see people for who they really are, the bleak times that gnaw at us, that we are who we are.

God wants us to love Him and others in the same way, but going on self-will makes us lose our path, and we forget to pray.

For others who are bitter like moldy old clay, beauty is but a word, and more often than not, it's never felt or even heard.

People have feelings and don't care to admit because someone may see them as weak and sensitive, or someone that needs to be controlled like a horse with a bit.

We learn from others as we go through life, from the beginning to the end, for our troubles and strife.

The empty heart can fill with love if we look past the exterior and take off the gloves.

This is so we can feel what we see, the inner peace that's in all God's creatures, especially you and me!

A Child's True Nightmare (Part II)

After leaving that home I was pretty well traumatized. I say this because I only remember lying down in the social worker's lap and the rest was a blank until I was brought to the other home. These people were really nice and I was under the impression that my mother would be coming to get me in two weeks. Well two weeks turned into three, then four and eventually they said she was never coming back. Needless to say I was heartbroken and homesick. I began to question my new family why my mother wasn't coming to get me when they said that she was. They said that she didn't want me anymore and that she was giving me up for adoption. This didn't sit well with me at all. It was so overwhelming I began to develop a very bad stuttering problem.

They thought I was doing this for attention; really? I didn't even know what it was, let alone fake it. It got so bad they were frustrated to the point of yelling at me every time I opened my mouth and screaming at me to stop! Their own kids began to make fun of me. I remember shutting down and not wanting to say anything, which made matters worse. Now I became a problem to them. Later on through a desperate attempt to find my Mother, they finally understood that the stuttering was a result of trauma; it wasn't an act. You have to understand that the case worker, when she found out that the woman had been beating me, had no idea about being locked in the closet naked, beaten near to death, lying in my own excrements, the salt, the bleach, the death threats and of course the rat! She never told this family anything, so as far as they knew I was just a child being given up for adoption. This goes on even to this day. I think if you are going to place a child that has gone through what I did or worse needs psychological help before being placed in any home.

I don't know how long I was there, but I know it was long enough for the many chain of events that added to my list of nightmares throughout my adult life. At this point of my stay for the most part I had accepted that my Mother wasn't coming back, but subconsciously the trauma still remained and the memories were still alive. These thoughts sparked my bold nature and my sincere desire to find my Mother. Down the road from where I lived there was a school bus stop, and everyday I would go there to see my foster brother and sister off to school.

One day I stayed there a little longer than I should have and other kids started showing up that were just a little older than I was. Soon another bus showed up and they all started getting on and I followed right behind them without the bus driver saying a word to me. I didn't know where I was going, but I thought maybe I could recognize something that would help me find my Mother. The bus made many stops picking up kids I didn't recognize. I didn't even know where the other kids were that I was talking to; there was so much noise, I was confused. The driver eventually dropped them off at school and I stayed on the bus just staring out the window. Pretty soon I noticed that we had been traveling many miles and I was starting to get hungry, so I walked up to the bus driver while she was at a stoplight and asked her if I could go home now. I startled her, she asked what school I went to and I told her I didn't go to school.

She then asked me where I got on at and I told her I didn't know. So she took me back to the school and the principal gathered all the students in the gym to see if anybody recognized me. Someone did and he knew where I lived. It was one of the older kids that I would talk to in the morning and I began to cry. I remember him hugging me telling me not to worry. He asked me why I had gotten on the bus and I told him I was trying to find my Mother. This started a relationship with him because of my boldness to find my Mother. When they brought me back to where they picked me up, my foster parents were there along with some other neighbors that had been looking for me since early morning and it was now a little afternoon.

When they saw me.they were immediately.inquiring where I was and I could see they were genuinely glad that I was there and alive. I told them why I had left and that I wasn't pretending about my stuttering problem. Their reaction helped ease my pain and accept them as part of my new family. The parents understood but their kids still had a problem with my stuttering as most kids can be very-mean and unforgiving. They made me feel lonely at times which I felt unwanted and it was hard to remember that they wanted me to be part of their family; I guess it was better than being locked in a closet starving and dying. As each day passed I started to accept more and more that my Mother wasn't ever coming back to get me. My life seemed pretty normal I guess except for a couple of major incidents that I am lucky to be alive.

For instance; there was this time where I was riding my tricycle down the side of the house and it was summertime, the grass was short and dry. It had a real steep grade that ended at the seawall that had a fifteen inch step in front and a three foot flat surface; on the other side, nothing but the ocean bay. I tried riding down the hill with my shoes on but it inhibited the speed that I required.

So the next time, I took off my shoes. As I gained speed I noticed I was going a little too fast so I put down my feet hoping to slow me up a little but found that the friction made my feet bum. I tried again, but it really hurt, so I Just lifted my feet and went for it. Before I knew it, the wall was coming so fast that all I could do was hope I didn't go over the edge. When the front wheel hit the cement the tricycle stopped but my body lunged forward smacking my face flush on the surface of the wall knocking out my front teeth and giving me a bloody nose.

I don't know what stopped me, because the speed I was going at I should have ended up in the bay which I could see just below me as my body was hanging over the edge from the waist forward. I hung there in the balance and slowly reached my arm back and inched my body sideways on the wall shaking like a leaf.

Now seeing red warm liquid pouring out of my face you can imagine the bloodcurdling scream that now was emitting from my expounding lungs. Picking myself up, I once again felt the fear of death, because I knew what would have happened if l went over the edge; as I couldn't swim. After I had gone to the dentist, he picked the broken pieces out of my mouth and stitched me up. I went home with my whole face aching once the Novacaine wore off.

The next morning I got up early skipping breakfast, and that goes without saying. I went outside to face my fears looking over the crash sight. I slowly walked up to the wall. As I approached the ledge I could see blood everywhere. I stepped up on the surface and inched my way forward. I cautiously leaned over taking in the depth from the top to the bottom.

You know, I never really had seen how far it was to the bottom, because I only remember the tide being in and the water always there. Suddenly my heart jumped in my throat making me recoil back to the lawn as I relived something from the past. Thinking of how close I came to death brought back a memory that I couldn't explain; but you all know what it is. Now what I'm getting at is this. We all hear of guardian angels and I know for a fact that they are real and I have three that protect me at all times. There is a short story that is a little bit later on in the book that will make a believer out of anybody.

Now continuing with the incident at the bay. Like I said at the time I had no idea where these feelings were coming from, but I know to this day that it was real and I will never forget it. That tragic event had kicked in another horrifying experience that brought on some new fears. Needless to say I was afraid of going too close to the bay; whereas before I used to run along the top wall without any fear of falling and now you couldn't get me within three feet of the edge. After a few weeks my mouth had completely healed and I was getting used to talking without my front teeth, but my stuttering still inhibited my speech. Since I wasn't as daring as I used to be, my friend was always trying to talk me into riding down the hill again.

By doing the stunt himself and of course with his shoes on, he made it look simple and safe trying to convince me at the same time. I humbly declined and it was followed by the usual childish remark; "chicken". I told him that I wasn't chicken and I said that I had a daring game we could play. He followed me into the basement where we had an old wooden ice box with glass on the doors that enabled you to see inside, or looking out from the inside which he was about to have a first hand experience at. He said, "Where's the scary thing you were talking about?" I pointed at the refrigerator and he said, "That's not scary". I opened the door and dared him to climb inside. He immediately took the challenge.

As soon as he was inside, I shut the door and walked away listening to him start to scream after just two minutes of me being out of sight. I waited for a couple more minutes letting him sweat for a bit after calling me a chicken. When I walked back over to the icebox I could see the terror in his eyes that were now full of tears as he pounded on the glass for me to let him out. I, of course, was demanding an apology and he quickly recanted his previous statement. When I opened the door he flew out like a jack in the box, running in all directions not knowing where to go. I was laughing; and he said he didn't think it was funny. He was really mad and said he was going to tell his Mother. He changed his mind when I said I would climb inside and he could shut the door, but of course I had certain demands like, you can't close the door all the way. He started to walk away saying he was going home. I agreed to let him shut the door and that quickly changed his mind.

After a few minutes I said, "Alright that's long enough, I want out now"! Naturally he stood there laughing like I had. That's when I got very serious and told him if he didn't let me out right now I would beat him up when I got out, and he knew I was serious from past experience. He opened the door and I was very furious with him shoving my friend down onto the cement floor. He started to cry and I helped him up by telling him I was sorry. He decided to go home at this point, and I didn't stop him. I myself wasn't finished with the game yet.

I crawled inside and shut the door as far as I could, I pretended to be locked in, but the door being partially open just wasn't the same. So I opened the door all the way again and pulled a little harder this time, just barely getting my hand out of the way of being smashed and the door slammed shut. I immediately tried to push the door open, but I was locked in and I began to panic. I remember the top of the icebox didn't have a handle, all you had to do was pull it open. I tried to reach up through a small gap between the lower refrigerator and the upper part. You may not believe this, but I remember measuring with the length of my arm to see if I could open the door slightly, at least so I could get some air.

As I stretched to my limit opening the top just a little, my body temperature was increasing from my fearful demise, the glass began to fog and I remember a soft voice saying, "Conserve your air, don't panic". It was very cramped in there because of the way I was sitting, so I tried to reposition myself. In the process the glass began to fog up again and I felt a little woozy, so I stopped shifting and laid still. It had been a long time since I'd been in there and I felt sleepy. I was just about to close my eyes when I saw my foster Mother starting to hang some wet clothes on the line and I started to pound on the glass with my feet which I couldn't do very hard because I didn't have much room to move.

She stopped what she was doing and went upstairs. I thought to myself, "Why didn't she come over and open the door, didn't she hear me"? I started to feel a little sick to my stomach and a little lightheaded as terror was setting in. The fear I felt two weeks ago was coming back and my situation was beginning to feel hopeless. Just then I saw my foster Mother again, just barely through the lightly fogged glass and this time I didn't care if my air ran out I kicked with all that I had left and began screaming. I had to stop. I felt like I was going to pass out, and then I saw the basement light go out and she was gone again.

I remember thinking to myself, "Was she like the other woman, was I being punished for locking my friend in the icebox, was she going to let me die in here?" The air was so thin now and I was about to go out. All of a sudden the door opened. Feeling the fresh air, I deliriously sprang from the icebox shoving her out of the way running around like my friend had done, except I was a little more out of it. I even remember asking her why she didn't let me out, I couldn't breathe, didn't you know I could have died in there; I was in there for an hour, why didn't you let me out? She said, "I couldn't have been in there that long you would have died".

Well I knew better, because it was daylight when I went in and now it was dark outside; you make the call. From that point on I didn't trust her anymore. My child-like mind was uncertain whether she saw me in the icebox or not. I knew one thing for sure I wasn't going back in there no matter what, and now my trust level had gone back to zero. To my recollection in less than a year, I had reached near death three times, and now a fourth was rounding the corner. I don't know how long it was from this incident to the next, but it wasn't long after. It was the weekend and we were at some kind of club, or someone's house that had a swimming pool. I remember there were several families and lots of other kids varying in age. Some of the other younger kids had life preservers on, but I had one of those plastic inner tubes that had a protruding seam that would chafe me every time I jumped in the pool. After a while I was trying to figure out how to jump in the pool.

After a while I was trying to figure out how to jump in the water without irritating my skin any worse than it already was. I found that by raising my arms a little instead of hanging onto the tube made it hurt less. I wanted to jump into the water full bore like the other kids, but it brought on too much pain. So I tried something different. I raised my hands above my head thinking I could catch the inner tube before I slipped through the hole.

This turned out to be a bad idea as it shot over my head. I didn't know what to do as I couldn't swim and I began to panic as I held my breath and started to sink. Suddenly I felt reassured as I felt my hands reach around my waist and I gasped for air when my head reached the surface and feeling safe I said,"Let's do it again". She said,

"I don't think so, what were you thinking, don't you know you could have drowned"? I said, "no I wouldn't, you'd be there to save me". As she climbed out of the water and gave me a hand out of the pool she said, "yea, but what if I wasn't"?

Not really wanting to take a look at the real message she was trying to convey, I shrugged it off by saying, "yea, but you were". About that time my foster Mother ran up to us asking if I was all right as she was inside when she heard what had happened. I boldly assured her that I was all right and not to worry. My foster mother, being very protective, decided it was time that I took a break from swimming. I didn't take this very well and I let them know it. Needless to say it didn't work.

It was late in the day and I was getting bored watching the other kids still swimming and I kept reminding my foster parents of that. Pretty soon all the other kids were starting to get out of the pool and I felt it was time for me to go back in, but they still weren't budging. Everyone was inside by now, but I was stHl outside looking at the pool that was smooth as glass. I wanted to go in so bad. Especially now since no one else was there, I would have the pool all to myself. I was full of energy and I wasn't about to give up; not yet. So I went back inside and found my foster Mother.

She was standing with a couple of other women and I walked up to her and tugged on her skirt. At first she kept on talking as I continued bugging her. Then she glanced down briefly as I asked her if I could go back in the pool. She was smiling at me as she looked back up and continued on with her conversation. I stood there for a couple of minutes and asked her again. The room was heavy with conversation and I don't think she realized what I asked her when she nodded her head yes in response to my question.

Now for those of you who have fallen short of this same situation, you should etch this incident in your mind. So many times were so involved in the adult world we neglect our children's requests and sometimes it can be fatal. Well getting the response I was looking for, I ran to the pool as fast as my little legs could carry me. I found my inner tube and put in on over my head. I ran it over my sides, the chafing reminded me of the pain I was going to experience if l didn't raise my hands over my head when I jumped in. So I looked at the still water and held my breath as I ran towards the edge and leaped forward, extending my arms determined this time to catch the tube before it shot over my head.

When I hit the water my confidence turned into panic as I started to sink seeing the tube above me as I tried to paddle towards the surface. I briefly remember thinking my foster sister would be there to pull me out, but as I looked towards the surface it was getting farther away. I remember still holding my breath as I stopped paddling my arms as I sank to the bottom. That was the last thing I remember; while I was alive. I heard someone say that I had to go back. I said, "I'm not done yet"?

The voice said I was going back and that it would help this family to understand something; I really don't remember much about it. I recall coming back to life in the back seat of the car laying over my foster sister lap and water shooting out of my lungs as I apologized for getting it all over her. She said it was okay trying to choke back the tears. They stopped the car for a moment asking me if I was all right. They said they couldn't get me to breathe, that's why they Were taking me to the hospital, but I told them I was fine. I was lying of course, my lungs hurt and my stomach was full of water. I tried to sit up and she wouldn't let me, she said I hadn't been breathing for at least twenty minutes not including the time I was in the water.

Like I said earlier, God had been running the show the whole time. I mean how many times have you heard of someone drowning and coming on their own without any assistance and expelling fluids from their lungs? Not in my life- time. When we got to the hospital they gave me a chest x-ray and found no fluid in my lungs, but my stomach was still full of water. So they put a tube down my throat and pumped my stomach; that was such a joyful experience.

When my foster parents told the doctor what had happened, I remember the shocked look on his face when they said that I wasn't breathing when they put me in the car and I came to on my own spewing water from my lungs. He said that was impossible. He looked at me and said you are a very lucky boy and all I can say is; God must have something special in store for you, because in my entire career I have never heard of anybody come back on their own like that. The nurse even said, "Gods got a plan for you". The doctor that examined me brought in other colleagues and nurses, seven in all to share this unbelievable miracle. I remember them just standing there looking at me shaking their heads in disbelief. Each one of the male doctors listened to my lungs for sounds of liquid and each said, "This is unbelievable".

The doctor said there might be some brain damage due to lack of oxygen for that amount of time. You know at that age I had no. idea what they were talking about; but growing up going to school I struggled just to maintain (c) average especially when I was a varsity football player in High School. You know I had even forgotten what God had done for me in that last home. This shows us as children how easy it is to forget that just a few months ago I was dying in a closet and promised to God if he got me out of that predicament I would never do to another human being what had been done to me. One thing that did change drastically was this family truly accepted me into their fold and my foster brother and sister stopped teasing me about my stuttering.

Months went by and the thoughts of my Mother slowly faded and I started to regain some normality. One day my caseworker showed up and took me for a drive and said she had something she needed to talk to me about. She said, "Well there's no easy way to say it; your Mother contacted me and she wants you back". She told me she didn't think it was a good idea to go back with her and that this family really liked me and wanted me to stay. Well I was so excited at the time, that family didn't even cross my mind, all I knew was I wanted to go home and nothing else mattered.

My worker tried everything she could to convince me that I was better off right where I was, but ultimately it was my decision and I knew what I wanted. This worker didn't know all the particulars of the horror's I endured from just two foster homes, or the put downs, the bus ride, the almost fatal ride down the hill, the ice box, and the biggie; the drowning. I mean the way my life was headed, what was next; being abducted and killed? You know the strangest thing happened on the way back to the house; I stopped stuttering. My worker noticed and could only attribute it to my Mother.

When we got back to the house my worker told them about my decision and that I had stopped stuttering and they were all surprised. I had to wait a week though, but that was okay, I was going home. That week they all started distancing themselves from me, I felt like I was back to the beginning with them. I just hope that they learned a big lesson from what had transpired while I was there. The night my Mother arrived my caseworker brought me out to the car and when I saw her I jumped into her arms and began to cry uncontrollably and so did she.

My caseworker sat there and all she could say was, "Well I guess I was wrong, you two belong together". Once again I don't remember leaving that night, I can imagine how that family felt. They had finally accepted me into their home and I chose my Mother who had abandoned me. But as a child, I wasn't thinking of their feelings, only what my empty heart was telling me. I soon had forgotten about the nightmares in the foster homes and we seemed like a family once more.

My Dad was still in the navy and we now we're living with grandmother and my mothers younger brother Bob in California. There was one event that I can never forget. Now most people when I've told them this story usually laugh or give you that look like; "oookay…", that's interesting. Most people don't believe in Satan and his demons, even people who have Christ in their life. What I'm about to tell you is real and it did happen.

My brother and I slept on the couch in the living room. Each night when all the adults were ready to go to bed they would carry us down stairs and put us on the couch, and most of the time we would be awake. I couldn't go back to sleep one night after being placed on the couch. I laid there in the dark for some time. Not wanting to be alone and afraid of the dark, I tried to wake my brother. There was no use; he was in dream land. So I lay there with the covers pulled tightly around my neck and stared into the darkness. My eyes soon adjusted, and now I could see the coffee table in front of me and the fireplace across the room. I decided to close my eyes and try to sleep.

Now this was not a dream; I opened my eyes a few minutes later and about halfway across the room stood a very small man; so I thought. He was dressed with a semi-pointed hat and a raggedy old suit that didn't seem to fit him. At this point he waved at me. I quickly pulled the covers over my head and hoped he would go away. After a few minutes I slowly uncovered my head and peered from under the blanket and he was still there but now closer.

"I have got to tell you all; I am getting the creeps right now as I write this and it is chilling me to the bone"! I lay there frozen; this was not a dream! This figure kept waving at me, smiling as he came closer. When he got to be about four feet away I ducked back under the covers again. I stayed there until I fell asleep. The next morning when I woke I told my brother about it and he convinced me it was a bad dream; but I know it was real!

The next night I made a point of staying awake. When they came to get me I played possum when they took my brother and I downstairs. I laid there for a little while and soon closed my eyes thinking; "maybe it was a dream". I know I was awake when I decided to open my eyes one more time before trying to go to sleep and there he was; much closer this time. He smiled and waved like before. I didn't take my eyes off him and I called out to my brother who would not wake up. So I pulled the covers over my head and started stomping my feet on the couch calling out to my brother.

He finally woke up grouchy, saying, "What do you want John"? I told him the man was here and he said, "I'm tired, go back to sleep, it's just a dream." I told him no it's not, just look. I heard him roll over and face the front of the couch and he said, "I see him! I asked him if he was still standing in front of me, he said, "No, he's right in front of me". I pulled back the covers and he was right, but it was the wrong one; because my man was standing right in front of me and I could see the other one in front of my brother. I was frozen with fear, were these real men? They were both dressed the same. My brother not being afraid of anything said; John you weren't dreaming he is real. I was shaking when I said, "mike that's not the one I was talking about, he's still standing right here in front of me. My brother said, ''He wants to shake my hand".

Suddenly I felt him lurch as if something terrified him. I asked him what was wrong; he didn't answer. I called out to him again; still no answer. This time he said the man's hands were so cold John; I'm scared. I hadn't looked directly in his face since he came closer, but I could see him much clearer now. He had a plump wrinkled face; his nose was very large as was his mouth while he continued to grin holding out his hand. I was hesitant at first, but his smile reassured me that it was okay to touch him.

I reached out and felt his skin, I recoiled and sensed the fear my brother had, and Mike must have snapped out of his silence as he called out to me asking me if I was all right. Shaking like a leaf and too petrified to even move; I told him I was okay as I held the covers tightly over my head. I described to him how his hands were as cold as ice. My brother agreed; that's what scared him. Being the oldest I told him to come down to my end of the couch and I would protect him. He said he couldn't move; he must have been petrified. So I asked him if he wanted me to come down there and in a weak voice he replied, "Yes' '.

Under the covers I knew they were just a few feet away watching me, and I thought any minute they would grab me, and I didn't know what these things were capable of. I kept going and I thought; why would they hurt us, they hadn't done anything bad so far; also my brother desperately needed me. It seemed to take forever as I slowly crawled on my belly towards Mike.

The couch was only about ten feet long. Now this part is what raised the hair on the back of my neck. I finally reached his end; so I thought. I felt the arm of the couch and lifted my head wondering where my brother was.

"Mike, where are you?" I called again a little louder this time…. "Mike!" He answered this time; "What!" What are you doing at my end of the couch? I thought you wanted me to come down there. He said, "What are you talking about? I haven't moved; I waited so long for you to come down here I fell asleep. I suddenly felt delirious, as I knew I hadn't turned around the other way; I was always going forward. I pulled the covers down.just a little more to see if the man was still there, my heart jumped in my throat to see that he was. Terrified, I covered my head so fast I began to shake; and feeling a little nauseous as I realized somehow he had turned me around without the slightest notion that he had done this. I don't know what prompted me to do this, but somehow! I remembered when I was locked in the closest dying and I prayed for God to get me out of there, and the feelings I felt when he did. I figured if he could do that, he could make that man disappear. So I prayed with boldness in my heart knowing he would not fail me. I can't explain how I know, but when I stopped praying I knew he was gone.

After that night they never bothered my brother or I ever again. I did try to get my brother to talk about it the next day and he didn't want to; he said it was a nightmare and he never wanted to talk about it again. A couple of years ago, I went to live with my brother and I brought it up and he had no recollection of this event ever taking place.

After some time, I guess my father had saved enough money and we moved into a rental house on Thompson St. in Portland OR. This place had its share of bad memories, mental, physical and sexual abuse. I recall very significant events that added to the nightmares and my violent defensive attitudes. I will cut to the chase and briefly explain about the somewhat good things that I can remember and a few of the violent ones. My father coming from a background of fishing and hunting had this on his mind a lot.

Most weekends were filled with watching my father make lead weights for fishing or tying his own flies; or whatever related to sports. Quite a few times his friends would be over drinking beer, which seems to be their favorite pastime. They would all give me sips off their beers and observe my transformation into a comical toy for their amusement. For sometime this was okay and my Mother didn't get involved. But one weekend she intervened and said that I had enough. Well this didn't sit well with me, because I wanted to entertain my father and his friends some more. To do this I needed more alcohol. The fuzzy feeling I was getting, it wasn't known to me. I somehow recognized it from previous times.

They all respected my mothers wishes and restrained themselves from giving me anymore. I remember going to the bathroom and closing the door, and on the back of the toilet sat a can of beer. I wrapped my hands around it and it was cold and full. I sat it back down and locked the door. I grabbed the beer and knew I had to guzzle the whole thing before anybody remembered they left it in the bathroom. The feeling hit me so fast, that's the last thing I remember until the next morning.

My Mom told me in later years that she found me passed out on the floor; I didn't even make it out of the bathroom!

Anyway, I woke up the next morning with my head pounding and sick to my stomach. I tried to eat a bowl of cereal and couldn't keep it down running to the toilet barely making it. Needless to say, that was my first hangover at age five. Oh, I forgot to mention, my Mother was the one who left the can of beer in there hoping I would do exactly what I did.

Things were smooth for a while up until the Columbus Day storm. It seemed like things started to fall apart as my Mother and father were constantly fighting, followed by her taking Dad out to the freeway with his bags, and my Mom crying all the way there. My Dad was always in his bed the next morning. This went on several times until one night he didn't come home, but he did show up where my Mother was working and wanted to come back; also he needed to borrow the car.

When my father came home, I was already out of school. He said Hi to me and went inside. After a little bit he came outside canying odd items like shoes, extra shirts and finally a suitcase. He walked up to me and told me he was leaving; I didn't know what to say. He stood over me and said, "John, you have to be the man of the house now and look out for your M9ther; she's going.to need all the help she can get". I started to cry and my father intervened with great words of wisdom for a five- year- old child that still had a lot of issues. "Don't cry, stand up and act like a man; don't let anyone get in your face, and if they do, you always make sure you hit them first and make it count. That was it; he turned and walked away and drove off with the car, wiped out the bank account and basically left my Mom with nothing and no means of transportation.

My Mother was in a financial bind and my uncle needed a place to stay; which was fine for a while. She was working two jobs to make ends meet; while our uncle watched us on the weekends.

One Saturday morning after my Mother had been cocktailing at her second job until the early hours. She was out cold and we all tried to wake her. Being the oldest and acting like a clown; I took one of her cigarettes and put it in my mouth and pretended like I was smoking it when my uncle walked and now my sister and brother had one in their mouths as well. He snatched the smoke from our mouths and said that it was a filthy habit and that we were in big trouble for smoking. As he was walking away I told him that we weren't smoking them, just pretending. He said, "Yeah, but you could have lit them and burned the house down". I told him that our Mother had taught us not to play with matches. My uncle said that we would resume this conversation when our Mother went to work. With only four hours of sleep my Mother was off to her first job. My uncle took us all to his bedroom and gave us a speech about smoking.

When he was done we all apologized except my sister who was only two and she really didn't even know why she was there. My uncle said, "I'm glad you all know that; now for your punishment. For an hour straight, you will each get 30 lashes with the belt every five minutes".

Now this is no exaggeration; I remember it like it was five seconds ago! My brother and sister didn't really catch what he had said, but I did and this was my child's true nightmare all over again! My uncle told us to take off all our clothes. Now I knew that this was going to be bad because I've been here before and I didn't know how my brother and sister would be able to handle it. He started with my brother and I watched as he swung the belt with fierce abandon. My brother tried to run from the belt but it was catching him across the back and legs through all thirty lashes. Without missing a stroke he started in on my sister and this made me sick; she was only two years old. This went on for a half hour and I looked at the blood running from their legs. He stopped, and then he said that he's going to take a break and would be back for the other half hour.

After he left l tried to console them and I thought to myself this has got to stop. I called him in and I said I wanted to talk to him. I explained how it was all my idea and that they shouldn't be punished any more. He agreed and sent them out side as he commended me for my Honesty and told me that I still had a half hour to go. When he came back from taking care of my brother and sister; the part that was so sickening was how nice he was, knowing what he was about to do. When the beating started I saw the viciousness that was in his eyes and the swing from the belt, this had me worried about the outcome at the end. Here I was again getting beaten until I was bloody! I thought it would never end.

When it came to the last five minutes my legs were shaking so badly, I wasn't sure if I was going to survive. You would think that most normal people would stop when they saw blood running down someone's leg; not my uncle! I believe he had a lot of pain in his life and he was taking it out on me. When he had finished he put my pajamas back on and made me stand in the comer by the front door the rest of the day. I stood there for hours looking at the blood that had soaked through and now had dried to my leg.

From the beating, if you can call it that, my legs were giving out from all the hours I had been standing. While he was in his room I would squat to rest my legs despite the pain. He would sneak down the hall just to catch me. He would stand me back up saying, "That's another hour young man. When he caught me the second time he told me that obviously I hadn't learned my lesson. He didn't remove my pajamas this time when he brought back the belt; maybe it was all the dried up blood, I don't know. I won't go into the beating this time, it takes too much out of me to write it; lets just say it wasn't even close to how long it was the first time, but just as intense.

A little while later my Mom called and he told her all about what happened. He failed to mention the beating my brother and sister received. I thought to myself, just wait till Mom gets home she'll see the blood on my pajamas and he'll be in big trouble. After he got off the phone he walked over to me and said that my Mom was coming home before her second job, and that I needed to change my pajamas. When my Mother got home she wouldn't even listen to me when I told her that he had beaten all of us until our legs were bleeding. She looked at my clean pajamas and said, "I don't see any blood, just stand there until you've learned your lesson".

She changed her clothes, and out the door she went. I started crying because I had a bad feeling of what I was about to endure tonight. For some reason my Mother had forgotten something and she came back inside and whist right by me. When she came out of the hallway and walked towards the door, I stopped her and pulled down 111-Y pajamas and screamed, "Look what he did to me"! I turned back to her crying as she said, "Oh my God son as she pulled my pajamas back up and told me to wait there. She went down the hall and I heard her scream at him telling him to get on the phone, because he needed to find somewhere fast. My Mother was appalled at what he had done to me. Oh, I didn't mention what she did when I told her about my brother and sister; she freaked out and told him to get out and come back later to get his things. Needless to say she had to call her work and miss a night's wages due to our demise because she had no one to watch us.

By the end of the evening my uncle had moved out. Days went by and we had a couple of sitters watch us; but the financial situation was weighing heavy on my mothers shoulders. She turned to my uncle who was staying with some girlfriend of his, and said that he would be glad to watch me. I'm really not sure where my brother and sister went, but I believe the neighbor may have taken care of them.

Anyway, when I found out I was going to my uncles I freaked. I was very frightened and told her I didn't want to go. She assured me that he would never touch me again. Well he never did; but another friend of hers did, but in a much different way that scared me for life, not letting any man touch me. He molested me on several occasions. He would always do this when I was taking a bath. I kept telling my Mother I wanted to take a bath at home, but she would always make me take it with her friends. I was crying my eyes out and yet she still didn't get it. So after a while I started locking the door and he would always want to come in, but I wouldn't unlock the door until I was dry and dressed.

I remember one morning he told me he wanted to show me some more like before, except he wanted to show me how real men do it and show me how they feel about each other. I told him no more, and if he did it again I would-tell my Mother.rle snidely said to me, "go ahead, no one will believe you". Well1 back then, he probably was right.

After that weekend something came up that couldn't have come at a better time. We couldn't afford to stay where we were anymore so my grandmother let us move in with her. It was crowded, but it was better than getting molested. Just like everything so far in my life, it had to come to and end.

One day we were all packed in my grandmother's car, which was huge by the way. There was my uncle, my Mother, grandma of course and the three of us. It seemed like a normal weekend drive with the family. We drove everywhere stopping every once in a while; they would get out and talk while we sat in the car. We eventually pulled up in front of this building and my uncle and Mother went inside.

They came out a few minutes later and they asked my brother and I if we wanted to take a tour of the inside. We both jumped at the chance just to get out of the cat. We had no idea. what was about to happen. Inside we met this bald overweight man that was just too cheerful, and he asked us if we wanted to take a look around. We both cheerfully agreed. We went down this long hallway and came to a door that opens like an elevator. The noise increased when the door fully opened. Inside were other children of all different ages. We started walking with him and I looked back to see if my Mother was coming too. I watched my brother start to run towards the door as it shut, flushing my Mother out of sight with its heavy metal mass. My brother stood there pounding on the door screaming for my Mother. This I knew for sure; it was a tour all right, a fair well tour. I went to comfort my brother and · told him that he was just showing us around, Looking up at the man I said, "Right mister"? He said, "I'm sorry but your Mother is giving you up".

You'd think by now I'd be used to this, but to tell you the truth. I felt like vomiting right then and there. I stood there holding onto my brother and looking at the stares I was getting from the other kids.

Now for those of you who don't know of this place it's called J.O.H., Juvenile Detention Center in Portland, OR. It is now a maximum security mini prison for minors. It was then too, but they put kids my age in here along with adolescent criminals and rapists. We were amongst very violent older children that had done various felony crimes. You know right now I really don't have the strength to describe everything that happened there; but I will say this, it was not a place for a five and a four and a half year old child to be in.

We were only allowed to go outside one day a month. We stayed there three months; and my memories of every morning having to mop up my urine from under my bed, because they would not let me go to the bathroom in the middle of the night still lingers throughout the deep recesses of my mind. They kept us in a locked room every night, and sometimes all day if there was a lock down. I didn't get to see my brother that often ·as he was always getting locked in his room.

I remember one day going up to my brother's door, which wasn't allowed when they were in lock down and spoke to him through the small paned window that had some kind of wire in it. My brother had cracked the window with his fist, as he stood there on the other side bragging how he did it and that he wasn't going to put up with the rules here anymore. And the hits just keep on coming.

Oh, I forgot to mention how my Mother would come every two weeks to see us and rip out our guts until one day she just quit showing up. Now don't get me wrong, I don't think that way now, I'm just writing how I felt at the time. And now as I'm writing this, I remember the day they were taking my brother and I to the same foster home, which was usually not the case, they would end up splitting siblings into separate homes.

This didn't last long as my brother had picked up some bad habits and wouldn't take guff off of anyone. I mean it was a constant argument with him, as he had to get the last word all while we were trying to go to sleep and he wasn't quiet about it. Well they split us up and for a week, we were both giving our foster parents a bad time about the split, but mine knew my brother had gone bad while he was there. They tried once more and I did my best to get my brother to listen; and I knew that first night trying to go to sleep it was the same thing again, "Did not, did too, did not, did too". Get the drift? Like I said that was then. I went through several homes before I found this older couple that I really liked. They were the Scott Family, they had one Son and one Daughter that were much older than I was.

They let my brother come and see me one time and he seemed like he had changed, he didn't seem as defensive. Time went on and soon I forgot about my Mother, l was accosted one day by this older boy who seemed nice as he swayed me towards this field that was out of sight of adults on a Sunday morning. We walked for a ways in the tall grass as he began to explain to me that he's taken many boys here and-what he was going to do to me.

At this point I knew I had to play along if I had any chance of getting away. I'd seen rapes before and I wasn't letting that happen to me. He pulled down his pants and as he lay down; that's when I ran as fast as I could and rode away on my bike. I looked back to see if he was coming and I didn't see him. Suddenly there he was from out of nowhere and quickly had a hold of my handlebars and was turning me around while still steering his bike.

He started taking me back down hill, I tried to pull away on the handlebars but he was too strong. I saw that he had all of his concentration on trying to control two bikes at the same time. He let go for just a second and I saw the chance; I kicked his leg into his bike and he went into a wobble then he bit the street. I stopped and turned around pedaling sluggish uphill and I saw this older man in his driveway and I pulled in. I told him about the boy and pointed at him coming up the street. The boy pulled in jumping off his bike as it slammed to the cement. He walked up to the gentleman and I heard him say distinctly, "What are you going to do old man, if you try anything I'll kill you, as he shoved him backwards almost knocking him down. That's when I got on my bike and pedaled at top speed since now I was on level ground. I got two houses away from my house and he pulled in front of me and I started screaming for help. He leaned down and said, "I know where you live and if you tell anybody I'll kill you and you won't know when I'm coming.

This guy had me spooked. Every time I would go outside I was constantly on the lookout for him, not straying far from the house. My foster parents noticed after a week or so and they asked me what was wrong. I finally broke down and told them about the boy. They were glad because they had heard rumors of the boy down the street that may have molested other kids and I told them what he had done and what he had said. He'll never bother me again, or anyone else for that matter.

Up to this point I've had my life threatened so many times by different ages, it was hard to find some trust in anyone. That's why when I got older, anyone who got in my face and wanted to chacha saw my anger fume to a level that no one could imagine. I would shake with rage and people could see that I had no fear and that I was serious when I said, "If you mess with me, I'll show you a side of hell that you've never seen before.

I remember one time where I didn't even start it between two guys that ran 260 lbs and the other about 230 lbs. After I had finished with them throwing them around like a rag doll, I stood behind the bar because this one guy was high on heroin and cocaine, he was still bleeding and wanted more. When she made the other two leave, I thanked her and she said, "you're 86 also and I asked her why, and she said, "I've never seen anyone's face change like that". I told her that everyone's face contorts when fighting. She said, "no John, your face turned into something that scared the hell out of me. I finally convinced her to let me stay, and to this day I haven't fought since, well not to that magnitude.

Now I'm not saying I'm the toughest around, not at all. What I am saying is this; I have been beaten down mentally and physically so bad all my life, I won't stop when someone threatens my well-being. I put up with the abuse from my stepfather and his friends until I was sixteen and I was bench pressing 280 lbs x 10 reps. We went to the garage and he looked at me and decided not to further this conversation. He never touched me again, but he had to keep up the mental abuse.

All the damage that had been done to me carried into my everyday living. In my mind, I was a loser, didn't try hard enough, and would never amount to anything. I took this baggage with me to the streets over and over becoming meaner throughout the years taking advantage of anything, or anyone that I could. The drugs and alcohol consumed as much of my life as possible. I stole from houses, stores, businesses, and whatever I could get my hands on to sell. My Mother watched me, and it broke her heart to see me like this, always giving me words of encouragement loaning me money once again knowing it wasn't for what I said it was. The drug would consume me over and over and always lead me back to the streets where I felt like I belonged. The gutter seemed to be my only answer, because I didn't feel my life was worth saving. Until one day I came to a place called Breaking Free Ministries. This is where I accepted Jesus while alone in my room and my foul mouth was removed as God showed me his grace and mercy for a wretched man such as myself.

I can't say for anyone else what he or she will expect when they let go and let God, but I can promise you this; he will never forsake you, I know that from personal experience. We are all different and he has a plan for every one of us; if we just listen to him and let him do his job.

LOST INSIDE ME

Looking at the past was a scary thought; it seemed like it would never end. Looking for God, I dropped my façade and decided to make Him my friend.

He made me laugh, He made me cry, and then He released all fears of how and why.

God knows me from the beginning, and He'll know me in the end. He showed me what's inside us all, and I truly found a friend, and I found it in me.

HE IS COMING SOON

So many children lost inside; they run and, they run, but they just can't hide.

Children, can't you see? God is everywhere; you just have to believe.

He's coming soon, and He's coming to clean; He's not like all the others, not stern and mean.

He's a loving God who will never let you down, so lift your head up high and wipe away that lonely frown.

God is good, and He is all the time; let Him stir your heart while you're still in your prime.

He'll keep you from Satan's sinful ways and keep your mind intact, and not in a daze.

Children, don't look at what your parents have done; we can't change their past. Just trust who died for our sins, the up-and-coming Son.

OPEN SAYS HE

Some say it's hard to be open and let others in because they're not ready to hear the truth, so they continue to live in sin.

I thought being open meant telling people where I've been and what I've done, but it's letting others show us the side that didn't work, the side that others had shunned.

This can't be accomplished if we continue to be in our own selfish gain, judging, criticizing, and not refraining from playing the same old games.

This is not a game with God; it's learning to be open and let your true feelings be your guide, to change your ways and drop that foolish pride.

That pride that used to beat others down when they confronted our childish ways; this is sinful and thoughtless, and it will be your downfall in the coming days.

If we're unwilling to learn from others, and we think we know it all, we're just fooling ourselves and be ready for a very big fall.

God teaches us to be free of our hypercritical ways by loving the Holy Spirit and the power of praise.

By lifting our hands and turning our lives to God, He'll massage those wounds that have become an inflamed façade.

So remember, it's not what you can memorize; it's how you walk in the ways of the Lord, that look that people see in your eyes, that freedom of life and the absence of fear that will soon be filled with peace when you let go and let God whisper in your ear.

NO MORE!

God, what's the matter with everyone? Have they all gone mad?

In the homes, in the streets, it's Satan's food of madness that these people eat.

The battered children, the battered wives, so much sin and pain that it makes me cry!

Satan is running rampant in his world domain, searching diligently for souls to gain.

You can see how many lives he's taken down, so many sad faces with long, evil frowns.

He's got a grip on about a billion lives, so many sufferings, so many lies!

God, I hope we can reach many lives with your words of law. The pain hurts my heart and rubs me raw!

Use me, Father, help me make them understand that we need to say no more and reach out with our hands.

Let me tell you something, I've been there, people. I can understand. But now I've returned from a sickly life of sin and crime, from drugs and alcohol, and the end of doing time!

Parents, can I give you some subtle advice? Don't beat your children for your mistakes in life. They can only learn by what they see. They can only become what you teach them to be!

Do you want them to fake their love that passes on and on to their children's children? Or do you want to see them live a life of love that will continue when you're dead and gone?

THERE IS LITTLE TIME, FOR I AM TIME

In life, there are two things that we forget: the things we know and the things we regret.

I've found through experience and God that the world is coming to a head because many believe that Jesus is dead.

Such blindness, a total disbelief; they see it coming and still feel no relief.

What does it take to make them understand that God wants to show them how to stand?

He cries with sympathetic tears when His people commit sin and crime, but still He stands by His word and allows us time.

The harp sings throughout the land as many people continue to complain and demand.

We see many crying in the streets as they wander foolishly, trying to acquire the food to eat.

The real food is the Word of God, the magical wonder of all things to come; for God says, "Ingest my fruit and do not veer from His words, or Satan will have his way and keep our eyes obscured."

In the end, there will be many things to see: the infinite light and God's truth through the many, for whom He is well pleased.

So look for the light across the sky and wait for God as you say your goodbyes, for in that time, for all who believe the ones who gave their sins to Jesus will see the one and only who died for you and me.

HIS GLORIOUS TASK

When the time is near and the callings begin, the chosen will be led to do battle against Satan, which they will ultimately win.

Countless many who chose not to believe will be shocked when they see others begin to leave.

They'll scream, and they'll shout for Jesus to save their souls, but for many, there will be nothing but deep empty holes.

It will be a frenzy of jealousy in the last days of their lives, for in the end, they'll see nothing but their lies.

It saddens my heart to know that many will die; I feel for those who cling to their gold, for it's nothing but yellow metal poured into a mold!

Be free from these monetary things; they are nothing but burdens and excess baggage you bring.

You have to be willing to leave everything you own to walk with Jesus, to be recognized and known.

For it's not what you have, but what you're willing to give for the freedom from bondage if you're willing to live.

A WITNESS TO YOU

This story is told by one who was bold and cared for nothing but what he could steal or be sold.

It begins from a life of abuse and pain, to many he met and nothing he gained.

His life all distorted, troubled with fear, he knew no reason and there was no cheer.

As many can attest, when we were young, we had no problems, this we confessed with our tongues.

But now as evil continues to poison this man, draining any good that was left, with a heart so cold and a punctured soul, he tries to stuff money into the many severed holes.

You see, we think that all we need is money and everything will be better. But guess what? Your life will always be a flop, even if you follow it to the letter.

As he lay there bleeding with his heart broken in two, God whispers these words that were few: "Do you remember the ones who witnessed to you? They were my chosen, for which I am well pleased. They brought you to me when they planted the seed."

"Now hear my voice and utter these words: Jesus is my Lord, come into my life, cleanse me of my sins, for my troubles and strife. Take my heart and soften my pain, for I give you my life, and my sins you have gained."

Now he was saved, anointed with hope, and it was time to do his deed, for now he was a child of God, to go forth and begin planting new seeds.

FOR MY SON

There will be a time when the saints will echo throughout the land, they will expand their joy for the coming of the Lamb.

The saints will march in an even sweep, while many continue to worry and weep.

Frightening thoughts come from the detached and afraid, the beast will devour those who saw no need to pray.

Many shall march in an endless line, preaching God's word to the countless who live like they're blind.

Though Satan will batter our weary shells, God will remain true with His love and keep us from the gates of hell.

Since the beginning of time, God fought our battles and won, and now He says in the end, "This one now… this one's for my Son!"

ONE OF A KIND BLOOD

When God made the heavens and the earth, He felt there was something missing, so He created Adam with no guilt or shame, just feelings of humility and self-worth.

God walked with Adam, while Adam listened to His words. God gave him everything, except a companion to be heard.

God, being so gracious and kind, letting His mind run free, He decided to create a woman made from Adam, His spirit, and the earth; this He made just for Adam to see.

Everything was according to God's perfect plan, but Satan's imperfection felt compelled to ruin the good that was inside of man.

When God had returned, He knew there was something wrong when He called out their names, as and they hid from God, because Satan had lured them, and now they knew all about shame.

This weighed heavily on God's mind, the beauty he instilled in their hearts was spoiled by Satan's jealousy when God relinquished him from heaven and told him he must depart.

Though many things had changed, God's plan never gave way, for He knew that one day there would come a time He would send His Son, and through Him, God would have something to say.

Even though His Son's miracles had everyone in awe, many couldn't believe that actually it was God that they saw.

Now, Jesus was one of a kind, just like Adam and Eve. His heart was pure, and His mind was clean, for He knew He would have to leave one day; this He had seen. He saw the torment and the torture He would have to endure, He saw thousands upon thousands of people He would heal and cure.

The many with disbelief scorned His beauty and His words, for the truth made them angry as they said, "He is no king, this is absurd!"

So they nailed Him to a cross, after beating Him near to death, but Jesus wept for all, with blood running from His side, for He knew this was His Father's plan, to cleanse the world with His blood as He died.

KNOWING YOURSELF THROUGH GOD

Uniqueness can blind your mind, making you think you're alone in your troubled time.

We sometimes won't admit when we're troubled with fear, so alone we sit with our past buzzing through our ears.

When our life gets on track, we try not to look back, but lo and behold, we still carry those heavy rocks in our sack.

The laden burdens of our past gone by, we've admitted defeat and, we still wonder why.

It's not for us to reason or wonder why we're here, just stop and listen, and soon you'll hear the words real clear.

The theory is very simple, if you pause and think it through, it's that old mystery trigger that grips our feelings, and eats at me and you.

Knowing the signs and why they are there can keep us sane and our hands from pulling out our hair.

The past has many triggers and a multitude of hands, so many itching fingers which come with fearful demands.

If we allow those demands to control our thoughts, Satan will step in and in his grip we will be caught.

So, when life gets intense, and you think no one cares, just ask yourself; do I really want to be alone with this one, or let God have it and be spared?

Know yourself and don't be blind, humble yourself before God and man, because God knows every inch of your soul and every line in your hand.

God can adjust your feelings that have their flaws, or when you mask your pain with a simple smile or facade. Be patient, look inside, breathe deep, and release that hot air you call your pride, and God will ease your pain and smooth out that bumpy ride.

MY DELIGHT FOR GOD'S WORDS

There isn't a day that passes by that I haven't heard confirmation of God's powerful words. For now, I see because my eyes are clear, not all blind and blurred.

It comes from the Bible, it comes from the church, it comes from the people I meet, and this food for thought I gratefully eat.

With God, I become stronger every day as He feeds me with his wonderful fruit it comes in waves that I continually crave that has saved my soul today.

At the end of each day, I feel like a newborn child that needs to be fed with a spoon, as I lay my head to rest with the call of the rising moon.

God's soft voice nurtures me with soothing words, I need this every day for my soul to be heard.

God has never failed me, but I did fail God many times in the past. I rejected the people God placed in my life, because my life was fit with a devilish cast.

I've noticed throughout my natural life, that if you don't feed the body the right foods, it will break down eventually, and soon it will fail you.

This goes for the soul. The Bible tells us to reach out for the words of God, become humble, and God will open the door. He will clear the darkness from your eyes, so you may see and stumble no more.

Is There Jesus in Your Heart?

I've found, since I accepted God and his Son, I see inside the faces of others how they think and how they run.

Some are too smart for their own good, they think others should think and act as they would.

Some think they can hide from God as they're looking for someone to control, but they forget God sees them so clearly, like a single fish in a bowl.

Jealousy is an evil trap; people can lash out at others with a thick leather strap. They lash out at the ones who are weak in the ways of the Lord, the ones who become frail, lazy, and bored.

These are the ones with "YE OF LITTLE FAITH," the ones with their foot still stuck in the door, the ones who profess his name but won't let God heal those open sores.

If we don't close those doors to the past, Satan will keep us sick and who knows how long it will last.

So boot Satan right out that door and change your ways because God is there, and he's still counting the days.

For you see, when the end is here, the lazy will snap with a cheer, saying, "Oh yes God, take me, I'm right over here."

But low and behold, God has seen the games they've played. God will pass them up while they stand confused and dazed, for God has seen all the many sinful days.

Though, others who prayed and changed their ways will leave as one, giving God all the glory and praise.

The sin will consume the others, and they will become deranged in their ways. They'll turn their heads from God and continue to do evil until God takes them away.

I, for one, am not afraid because I gave my life to God, and it was a freedom of choice I made.

It's a system of merit, there are many more deserving than me. I will gladly teach his words to countless others and show them what it means to be free.

Who's Running the Show?

Removing the cotton from my ears, this gives me time and the chance to hear real clear.

So many times I've heard before, take the cotton from your ears and stuff them in your mouth; I can do this now without running from the truth, as I listen to God, and He shows me how.

It's hard, I know, to say I don't know, but what does it take to be free? It's letting God do His work and teach you the ways, that the fruits of your actions are what you need today.

You say you're scared and you fear the unknown. Just ask the Lord; He knows, for He is the one who's really running the show.

It's humility in a simple form to begin a life anew. It's the ups and downs, not the ins and outs or the recipe for a fine stew.

It's the life we lead, and we must take heed, for now we know that God's in charge, and He's the one who's really running the show.

TURN IT OVER

Seeing violence all too often, it's hard to find some peace. I pull my feelings towards the top as God clears my head, and I feel the pressure pop and release.

He tells me my path has all been wrong, and I can't continue with my evil ways. I need to ingest His words to be strong in the coming days.

I'm not pure at heart, but I did give my life to Christ. I can express what God has done for me, but sometimes I wonder; what good does it do to those who don't believe?

There are those who think, "If I could just see God, this would help me believe." But this is one of Satan's lies that will deceive your mind and your innocent eyes.

Would it really make a difference if God showed His face? Not really. We would probably find it much easier to voice our complaints and express our views face to face.

It wouldn't really matter; we would still remain insane, pointing the finger and shrugging the blame, while acting innocent and playing the same old game.

Believe me, people, the time is near to add up the points and put to rest your doubts and fears.

Don't scoff at the believers because they can show you the way, a better life through Jesus Christ, and it can happen if you want it today.

God's Perfect Pitch

My walk with the Lord has brightened my life; I let others know why my eyes shine so bright.

I've been so busy, so selfish, so filled with me, I forgot God's purpose… to help someone find their way to Thee.

When I least expected it, God pitched me a perfect pitch; He put someone in my way to help me get out of my ditch.

I learned I was living as only one player in His grace; now I include all, all of God's race.

God has shown me His love; now it was time for me to show someone my love.

God has taught me so much, that through others my heart can be touched.

A handshake and a smile, a pat on the back; the words from God to shield against Satan's attacks.

By God throwing me a heavenly pitch, I can teach another how God's words can make us feel rich.

I know I can do anything with God by my side, even stand against those who won't drop their pride.

I've taken a challenge, another leap of faith, to care for someone besides myself; for this is God's undying glory and grace.

LET ME EXPOUND YOUR NAME

When I'm alone and feeling down, I look to the sky, and it wipes away my lonely frown.

When my smile returns and my head is filled with joy, I'm alone with my God as I whisper His name, and He gives me strength to deploy.

Just knowing He's there in my times of need, I heedfully enjoy fulfilling His deeds.

To think of returning to the walking dead is so far from my mind, it's hard to even consider or conceive, the memories of being distraught and blind.

I like whispering your name when we're all alone; I know I don't need to shout and raise my tone.

I used to raise my voice and shout your name, but it was out of rage, and a way to vent my anger and shame.

Now, when I profess your words and others are around, I don't whisper your name or hold my voice way down.

I don't care what others may think because I want everyone to know how I feel, that my faith is strong and my faith is real.

I have a message for all to hear, that I have become a link in God's massive chain; this has been built from people who lived in shame, without the word, they were slowly going insane.

We used to live in a world of sin, but now we live by example, to tell you all of our return and where it all begins.

THE POWER OF PRAISE

The power of praise was shown to me; I saw how it worked and how it set many sinners free.

Behold the power of prayer; to some, it seems like work, but to me, it shows God's awesome love, and to others, it's just some strange little quirk.

Using the power of praise on those who stray, it always seems to heap burning coals upon their days.

Then there are those who are really lost; it sets their souls to blaze; their minds become confused and blank because they're always looking for easier ways.

I've seen it work so many times, to some, it saves their lives, but to others, it bites their hands and catches their little white lies.

When I see this happen, I raise my eyes in awe that my eyes have seen God's glory and grace; to His truth, I see no flaws.

ASK AND YE SHALL RECEIVE

We think and react on our own self-will, to gain new knowledge for our empty holes to fill.

We pray, and we pray, thinking of things that we want, while Satan does what he can with his subtle little taunts.

He can frequent our minds, telling us we can do it on our own, but in our hearts, we know it's a lie; we've tried, it's been shown.

The more we ask God for His benevolent love, the cleaner our heart becomes, like a pure white dove.

He is pleased as we hand Him the key to our hearts; He opens our minds and commands the evil to depart.

It's a slow process changing the tapes in our heads, but the more we feed our soul with thoughts of good, the more it becomes part of us like a tightly-knitted hood.

Of course, we're reminded by the bad days gone by when we think of the kind of life we've lived, and we wonder why as mist forms pools in our eyes.

To be set free from the many worries that self can bring, all I can say is, "I'm excited when I shout, 'PRAISE BE TO GOD!' and my soul is buoyant while I sing."

It's very simple, except for the complicated mind. I believe if God were right here, He would say, "Be not afraid, quit clinging to your old ways, and I'll smooth those edges that were so jagged and frayed."

Those edges were so sharp, the cuts they made were deep; they kept the pain continuing, and into darkness, we coldly creep. Until we're free of being our own self-sacrifice, nothing will ever suffice. But God can remove our pain, to close those open wounds, and heal the bloody stains.

He shows us what is right and what is real; all we have to do is lift our hands to God and kneel.

SIN OR SCORE

I've been around this old world for many years, not more than some, but I have oiled a few gears.

I'm coming to learn when the Holy Spirit says no, this is what it means, and don't mask that thought with, "Hmm, I don't know?"

A sin doesn't necessarily have to be against someone else; it can be so simple, it can be against yourself.

I know it's hard to keep away from where we've been; just ask God for the strength not to sin, and let Jesus be your coach, and He'll take you to a victory and win.

Here's another way to reach that goal, and there is no trick; just ask God to make that score, to reel His mighty foot and make that kick.

Once God becomes our point man, it's much easier to reach and obtain those goals; to become someone new, to grow and become whole.

Don't get me wrong, God doesn't expect us to be without flaws; He just wants us to obey His commands and abide by His laws.

If we remember to call on Jesus, God will sift through our sins and allow His Son to cleanse our souls and reset our pins.

THE RUNNING MAN

As I flee from place to place, I seem to be running around in the same old space.

Anytime I get mad and fear sets in, I pack my gear, so I don't have to hear what others are trying to stuff in my ears.

Sometimes I feel numb and dead, all I want is some peace and a place to rest my worried head.

Spirituality is like the common cold, it never grows old, it's always coming and going when we don't do what we're told.

This won't happen if we turn our eyes to Jesus and get down on our knees, then God can see us with our eyes full of liquid repent, the Holy Spirit to us, he has sent!

Now that my head is at rest, I have more time to be with God and become my very best.

Oh Father, teach me, test me, let me grow, show me how to give my heart to you and others and fight the evil Satan, my enemy, my foe!

NO LOVE LOST WITH JESUS

When love is lost, we exist without time, there can be no reason. Until we ask God to give us a sign.

Now it may not come as a blinding light or an angel in the night, it could be a mere whisper in your ear that will fill you with sheer delight.

When this happens and believe me it will, if you really want God, just listen and be still.

If you want what God has to offer and you're ready to commit, just give your life to Jesus, and he'll remove your sins as you serve and submit.

It's a love that no one can take away, it will remain with you always if you let Jesus lead the way.

For through the Father and his Son's return, they will comfort our hearts for what we have learned.

All they want is to give you peace and a willingness to live, for they know what we want and they're willing to give.

They remove all doubt and the worries disappear, they touch our souls holding us close as they whisper in our ear; …Shhhh, remember I'm always here, if you just ask me, there will be no reason to run in fear.

I'm coming, says Jesus, and the time is near, for you to feel my love and hold it oh so dear.

It won't be easy as you continue to stand, so just remember; I'll always be there holding your hand.

GOD'S WILL

God's will is perfect, there's no other way; he soothes our hearts while shaking our souls as we faithfully move forward and pray.

There's nothing like God's will, so impressive to see, the life he instills through truth and humility.

We ask with faith and know we'll receive, to be in Christ on bended knees. We ask Jesus to forgive us of any sin, so our hearts may be clean and God may begin.

God wants us to follow in his ways, and ask of his will to endure the days.

We feel him near us, and our souls encased, we feel his presence and his soft voice; we long to see his face.

When I pray and I reach to the sky I look up and I say, "I hope one day I can please you Lord and honor your Son, because you've strengthened my cord and my life you have saved."

God's will is perfect, a shining light, a love against darkness, not a nightly fight.

God's will is so prevailing he's even etched in rhymes, since the beginning of man, since the beginning of time.

So indicate to God what you mean when you pray, and he will make you unconquerable for everlasting days.

Pictures We Paint

We change and we grow as we begin to flow, through the mainstream or life that we know.

We accept and we dream, of peaches and cream, but to some it seems like sour grapes.

It's the acceptance of life, and the things we face, we look for the beginning as we learn how to trace.

This picture we perceive isn't a pretty sight, but what should we do, take a stand, or fight?

If we allowed ourselves to feel the pain, to suffer for Jesus, oh, the things we'd gain!

As we add more lines to the picture we paint, its rough areas seem so distant and taint.

We go through the motions, and keep ourselves in check, we go on living, but we never forget.

For this is a new beginning, a new face, a new life, a new place, for we need to make changes, and set a new pace, for this is love, and not a race!

A FAÇADE TO GOD

Sobriety is our gift to God, what we make of it can sometimes become a facade.

Thinking things through is what makes us grow, feeling your heart beating, oh how it flows.

If we forget we have a heart that beats steady and strong, it can turn on us and steer us wrong.

They say, "Follow your heart and don't listen to your head," because it will be a matter of time and we'll all wind up dead.

Once this happens and the ooze begins to fill your shoes, you must choose quickly before you lose all that you've gained and all that you've ever felt because soon the ooze will become hard and sticky, and then it will begin to melt.

Which shall you choose, a shade of darkness, or a patch of blue; I know what I would do!

Trying to decide which way to go, we often wonder, will it be easy, or will it be hard? Well, it all depends on if you're willing to ask God to deal you the right cards.

I've seen both sides now, and I'm ready to learn what there is to life and all about love and concern.

The child in me really wants to grow, but is deathly afraid of just letting go.

We've felt so much pain throughout most of our lives, that we can't imagine living without our little white lies.

So we continue to fight and hold tight to what kept us alive, feeding our flesh and always taking a dive.

Is it true? It must be, it kept us living and messed up all these years, through the good and the bad and the many, many tears.

It kept us bound to gloom and despair, as for the world, we just didn't care!

For in the past, we've been let down so many times, we felt there was only us, so we had to ring our own chimes.

Well, the scars of the past and the feelings of mistrust weigh heavy on our hearts like a bucket of rust.

I don't know about you, but I'm tired of failure and being someone I'm not, with my life all twisted and turned, like a log with a protruding knot.

I would like to begin by thanking God for always keeping me in His care, showing me His patience, and that He's always been there.

So please, God, remove my mask and take this ugly old facade from me, because I want to serve only You, and serving You is the only way there can be.

A WALK IN TIME

I look back at how I walked in life, I see the discontent I had in my step; no wonder my life was a mess, and into darkness I always crept.

My walk was heavy, so lost in life, I searched endlessly for some faith in flight.

I ran from time, all covered in sweat, the nightmare knew no end it would never let me forget.

There were no reasons, and there were no rhymes, all I knew was sinful shame and crime.

My mouth was foul and full of lies, I hated all that was good, and to all I saw in my eyes.

For I was lost, and couldn't be found, a wandering soul that was earthly bound.

Caught in the clutches of the evil ways, just biding my time and counting the days.

There was no time where my life was concerned, because I felt no purpose, for I had not yet learned.

The lessons of life are for all to see, to fulfill the experience of our ultimate destiny.

The trials of life are full of heartaches, anguish, fear, and fright, but no one can stop you from the dead of night.

For this was my walk for all to see, the walk of a man so blind, and this was all meant to be.

We all have our walks, and we learn from our mistakes, this is our life, but it's not for us to take.

We can continue to walk with the blind or surrender to God, and He'll show you a sign. But if you're still blind when you ask for His help, all you'll receive is what you perceive, and as much as you're willing to believe.

There can be no reservations where the Lord is concerned, for He knows what's in your heart, and what you're willing to learn.

I tell you what I've learned, and that's to tell others what they may receive, to share my wisdom that God is good, and if they truly believe, God will do all He says that He would.

We can't make evil walk with the Lord or make evil repent, but once evil has no hold anymore, we can lead others toward God's heavenly door.

For there are those who will continue to do wrong, let them do wrong; there are those who will continue to do right, and let them do right; let those who are holy continue to be holy, for they are God's servants, and they are doing what is right.

AWESOME POWER IN JESUS

I feel love today, like none I've ever felt before. It's a feeling I've resisted in the past, while running from heaven's door.

He's waited so long for me to be strong and ask Him for every need. He showed me love and His wondrous words as I carried God's message, doing His many deeds, like the story of Johnny Apple and what he did with the seeds.

I feel God's sweet touch, and to me, this is real because I know He's there and how He makes me feel.

Satan has tried so hard to obtain my soul, to keep me down, filling my head full of bitterness and mold.

He'll tempt me, he'll trick me, and never let me forget of the horrors I've lived that were so easy and set.

But Jesus has control, and I truly believe that I have a new life, this I now perceive.

It's not a hoax, nor chance, it's God's divine power that leads this dance.

It's faith, it's healing, it's truly joy to see us as miracles and not one of Satan's little toys.

Jesus extends His arms and gives us a hand when we can no longer hold our heads high or can no longer stand.

He's a loving spirit, and He guides our hearts to free our souls that have been torn apart.

I struggle no more inside myself, looking for someone who wasn't there. That someone was me, who wanted to see what it was like to walk with Jesus and to truly love and care.

THE OTHER SIDE

We see life in a different way, and there are things we can't explain, to others or ourselves, of the haunting pain.

Will people mock us, push us away, or will they embrace us and let us grow to see another day?

Skeptics eye us, and others laugh, we look for others who know of our past.

They're few to find and not in demand, you can't find them in the paper or look for them in the stands.

Are we afraid of what people might think, are we crazy for what we know, that we've truly been with the one who really runs the show?

God doesn't have to reveal Himself to me because I know that He is real, and I don't have to see to believe.

I hope others like me can relate to what I know, what's keeping God's secret will make me want to say, "why can't you understand, what's not to believe; trust me, there is a new life when our time is up, and we have to leave."

I will be Gentle with Myself

Hush, the lonely child; a need for comfort from torment through a life of beguile.

We live in the past, thinking we've forgot, but it comes out in our speech and definitely in our thoughts.

As we become of age and our parents say, "Act like an adult," so we say, "Why, so I can grow up to be just like you, a person stiff and stern, a wise guy?"

Parents, don't you realize what you're doing? You're depriving your children of the right to be children, to learn and grow, to make their own mistakes without feeling like they're worthless and low.

This is what we carry through life on our backs, that heavy-laden burden that Satan will continue to add more rocks to your sack. When the weight becomes too much, we need to vent our heavy load from what we've been shown and told, and now our heads are about to explode.

We say to ourselves, "Why should I carry this heavy burden all by myself? I know, my children should share my miserable thoughts, I'll do what my parents did, except I'll start when they're tots."

Oh, this guilt we carry, this message we send, we're so trapped in shame we can't even be our own best friend.

I've seen so many who say their life is just great, but I feel their pain and I see their hate. They're caught in self-gain, more money, more power, more self-control; I don't think so, they're just digging a deep hole to hide their true soul.

You see, we think of ourselves as being this great person of care and concern, but on the outside, others see us struggling to hold back the tears of pain, for what we might learn and what we're unwilling to gain.

It's not that we don't want these true feelings of joy, it's held back by some angry girl or boy. These thoughts are locked deep in our minds, the ones that tell us it's weak to be kind.

Don't be afraid to pull up that dark shade, it feels so much better walking in the light of day. God just wants you to feel His love, so give up your will and the mistakes you've made.

Remember this when you feel all alone; maybe, just maybe, that's when God wants you all for Himself and also to yourself be known.

CLEAN YOU HEART AND THE MIND WILL FOLLOW

The cement jungle can tangle our minds, it traps our souls, it's the sign of the times.

It teaches us the fearsome ways of the land, to hate one another, to take what you can.

We point the finger, we mock, we judge, we laugh, we attack each other with a sharp pointed gaffe.

Each nation says be kind to your own, but we see them fighting and killing each other, for what we don't know.

I see the gangs marking their territory, like a dog does to a tree, they're killing in sprees, and soon they won't care about anybody, even you and me!

It's like no one wants to budge; "you say this, I say that, well, if you give me this, I'll give you that."

What a childish way to live, to always be taking but unwilling to give!

We need to stop and see who's to blame; it's not you, and it's surely not me; it's Satan laughing from the sidelines in this violent game.

The sooner you see this, the less power he has, for a clean mind is clear, and impossible to razz.

You say there's no hope, you say it's no use, I beg to differ, and I'll make a bet with you!

Because I found a way to release my pain, to my Father and His Son, my sins they did gain.

When I let go, and they cleaned my mind, they showed me love, and my heart I did find.

I heard it pump, and it was slow at first, but once I gained strength, my bubble of hate did burst. Oh, what a relief and the feelings of joy, you can't imagine what it meant to this lost angry boy.

To feel His presence and sense His touch, to think I could care and love this much.

If you've never experienced this world of joy, you'll remain in the dark, a scarred angry little girl or boy.

So I'll make a bet that you'll never regret; that you're not tough enough, to let God help you forgive and forget!

GOD'S LOVE AND GRACE

God says, "Have I not commanded you to be strong, to hold your faith with courage, even when the days may seem long?"

The Lord tells us, "Do not be frightened or dismayed, for He will always stand by our side, even when we're lost and afraid."

He keeps His love in your heart, as the old ways subside, the Lord will always be there if you just let Him be your guide.

He says our bodies are His temples, do not conform to the ways of the world; transform your thoughts, renew your mind, test your courage, be pleasing and kind.

These are His words, His perfect will, etch them in your heart, and soon He'll instill the true meaning of His grace, and His love you will feel.

There are those who know nothing of God, but God knows about them, that's why He has us to pass on His fruit from our mighty stems.

God's love is our sap, and we, that are strong, should bear many fruits as the days go on.

Our Lord Jesus Christ, Himself and God, they loved us with their grace and taught us to refrain from malice and facade.

God's grace gave us encouragement and a faith to plant the seed, that we may be strengthened by His words and even more by doing His deeds.

As we wait for His return, and the coming of His Son, we stand with hope and courage and strive to be joined as one.

SATAN ROARS, SO YOU WON'T DEPLORE

There are those who don't believe that Satan exists, they are the ones who will tempt others to refuse and resist.

They believe all the lies that will show in their eyes, as Satan will show you that you have to get all that you can before you lye down and die. Now, if you're caught in this pitiful demise, you will covet from many and snuggle with darkness that you should despise.

It's a ghastly world of hate and fear, the demons know their end is coming, yet they take from many and still they jeer.

The roar of the lion makes our hair stand on end, as Satan rears his head and mumbles his voice; for he has no teeth to spit out his treacherous lies pretending to be your friend.

We should be confident in our faith, God tells us in his own words; we should be innocent of evil, for this he has reassured.

The seductive jealousy of wanting more, fills the minds of many while Satan fogs your eyes, so you're unable to deplore.

Now deplore is a word that means expression of sorrow and regret, Satan despises this word, because he makes you think it's weak to show true repent.

I have now found through weakness that love replaces fear, but I also fear for the many; "for the ones that are afraid to face God and look at themselves in the mirror."

TWO PATHS

There are two paths that we can surely choose, if it's the wrong one, we can most assuredly lose.

We can choose the path that we know so well, it's so familiar that one is hell.

Some think that you have to die to go to that awful place, but guess what, it can be right here and in your face.

This happens when we're all alone, feeling miserable because we haven't been shown.

It's the path that Satan paints with the truth and it's really a lie, there is hope if we just ask God to get us off that path, that path of lies.

This path that keeps us blind to God's true words, it will only keep us insane and our lives obscured.

If you look at your life and how it's gone, can you really say it's that great, or has it all been wrong?

How can it hurt to go down another path and try something new, to truly be one of God's children, one of the chosen few?

When Someone Has Fallen

Oh Father, it saddens me so to see someone fall from your grace, someone who has professed your words to people of all your race.

When they say they've tried God and it didn't work, this can only mean one thing: Satan has stepped in with his worldly lies, and with this, madness and desperate sighs.

Oh Father, they've lost the key, the key that keeps Satan from spreading confusion in their minds and sending them on wild rampant sprees.

Oh Lord, I profess to you that I am weak, and I ask for your loving grace. Help me stay strong when Satan does me wrong, for I need your Son by my side when he gets in my face.

As I hear Satan's lies, I can imagine his eyes. I stand fast as I unload the holy glare with words of grace, for this I know, God's words will fill Satan's empty space.

Oh yes, Father, I can do anything while you stand by my side, because I did the smartest thing: I handed you my foolish pride.

As I pray and confess my sins, I need your strength always, for whenever Satan attacks again.

So keep me weak, but make me strong. I profess your words and expound your love as the days go on.

THE BATTLE BETWEEN GOD AND EVIL

The forces of evil are smeared with brilliant colors, like the coral snake and all the poisonous others.

Like the many things in life, they can paint a pretty picture, but it can't make you wander as long as you know the scriptures.

Sometimes we predict what we would like to see and make our minds justify the outcome of an unreal fantasy.

Illustrious blues, crimson reds, they fill our eyes, they fill our heads.

Is it really what we see, or a pretty package hiding sinister thoughts of broken dreams?

You see, Satan lies and tells you it's okay, but if you would listen to that small still voice, it would tell you, "No, don't do it, you know it's wrong. Just call on me, and I'll show you the right choice and make you strong."

But if we're still caught in sin, we try to manipulate that small voice and believe what we want. Then that choice will mesh together into a reality, and Satan will win.

We must battle the enemy of this world and take a stand, to be God's children and lend others a hand.

The crusade is just beginning in the war on sin, to stand together and not look back on the way we've been.

Stand tall, stand proud, and shout out loud, "Satan, I've seen your colors that you used, and no longer can you control my life and make me sing the blues!" I know you're the ruler of this realm, but I have another who steers my path, and man's my helm.

You know who He is! The One who loves me and is the giver of all good things, and from my heart, I praise him daily and joyfully sing.

OPPRESSION

There are spirits in this world that we just can't see, the ones that can oppress all human needs.

Now the needs are very simple if you know where to look, they're in all God's people, and especially in His book.

But there are many who depend on themselves and friends, that they refuse to ask the One who can truly mend; that One is Jesus, your one and only true friend.

I have found, through time and the power of prayer, that God is the answer when we're running scared.

You see, the spirit of oppression is so subtle in its ways, that it can confuse your mind and keep you in dismay.

It keeps you oblivious to its draining power, that it becomes part of you in every waking hour.

God has shown me, in my times of weakness, that it attacks your soul and removes your meekness.

It's so deceiving, that when the spirit is approached, it will recoil and become angry; making you think it's a hoax.

But the truth be known in God's own words, we should listen to the ones who know we've been lured.

These are the ones who can feel the demon spirit by your side, the ones who know that the spirits can lie.

But if the soul is captured and held in its grip, it won't release its hold because your will has been stripped.

So when someone sees you and tells you you're under attack, be open to their words, for God wants you back.

EVILS WEAR A SMILE

It says in Second Corinthians Chapter 11:13-14, for such men are false apostles, deceitful workmen, masquerading as apostles of Christ. And no wonder, for Satan himself masquerades as an angel of light.

It is not surprising then if his servants masquerade as servants of righteousness. Their end will be what their actions deserve!

Now God has let me learn from my mistakes; and in His words, He says, "Always test the spirits and you can't be led astray, for I am the final word, and fear what I say."

But being human and a newborn in Christ, a smile and a kind word can surely feed our flesh, and God will observe to see if we pass the test.

The test being from Satan since the beginning of time, his flattering words and a crooked smile can surely mislead the blind.

Now I'm not saying that we're blinded by the light for which Satan fills our eyes, but the fact that we as believers can wander from the flock, being devoured all alone as we silently cry.

Once led astray, they'll shower you with praise, as time goes by, they'll smile as they weave you into their evil ways.

With our backs against the wall, there's only one way out, to rebuke those demons, letting go with a hearty Holy Spirit shout! "I rebuke the bind that you hold over me, and I ask the Holy Spirit to reveal the truth, so I may truly see." This can only be accomplished by having the truth etched in our hearts, and remembering Paul; who God gave His grace to the biggest sinner of them all.

So remember, just call out to God, He's holding your crown with love in His heart. He wants you in His standings, not all lost and torn apart.

ARE YOU CLEAN?

We come from a past from which many have seen, a living hell of madness; and now before Jesus, we submit our lives to coming clean.

We repent for our past when we were ruthless n' mean, it wasn't our fault; Satan dirtied our minds and kept us from becoming serene.

Satan waved things in our face that fed our flesh, a burning desire that kept us dwelling in an infested nest.

No matter how we tried to forgive our sinful lives, Satan was there chattering in our ears, making us think we were no good, so our hatred would build and build, and it showed in our eyes.

Deep in our hearts, even though we still sinned, there was always a spark of life that wanted to return to the way it was when we first began.

There's a spark that is in all of our hearts, Satan will keep it all covered and wet, for a fire can start from the smallest regret.

Some of us manage to make that spark ignite, to shake our fists at Satan and say, "adieu, so long, and good night!"

For we're tired of living like mad dogs on the run, lashing out at others who are happy and having fun.

So when we come to know God and accept His Son, we live with God's word and we stand as one.

But many can attest in our lives, we have characters in which we call defects, we carry these into church like heavy chains around our necks. In Galatians Chapter five, it says, "Are you walking in the Spirit, or are you living while you're still dead inside?"

We would all like to believe that when we were saved, that our minds would be erased, and it would be easy sailing in our future days.

But there are trials and lessons to be learned, to live a life of love, with peaceful thoughts and concern.

"Oh yes, we go into church every week and we say, I truly believe, and I am truly saved!"

But we're seen by our brothers and sisters' eyes as we try to convince ourselves that we are truly clean, but is it the truth or one of Satan's lies?

I ask you again; are you clean? Can you honestly say that you walk the talk, or will you admit to Jesus that you have sinned and your mind sometimes strays?

I can truly say and admit this fact, that I slip from time to time, and my mind can surely jump off track.

The more mistakes I make, the more I learn when I'm slacking in God's holy ways, this is when I ask for wisdom to detect my sinful actions when I stray.

For when I'm not clean, I feel disorganized and distant, not calm and serene.

When I asked Jesus to cleanse me with His blood and I handed Him my heart, He redeemed my soul, and now the evil must depart.

Our pride sometimes doesn't want to admit that once we're saved, that our lives can lose track, and it's just a matter of time, and we'll start to fall back.

This is where Satan will try and convince us that it's okay to make mistakes without any repent, and God will understand and give us a break?

I ask you again, "are you clean?" We need to become weak and humble ourselves before God. He knows we're not perfect, that's why He sent His Son, to redeem our souls, to probe our hearts as we lift our hands praising His name, and ask for forgiveness; as God hugs our hearts and removes our shame.

<u>*Byron Alexander*</u>

Here are a few poems I've written about mankind and nature. Please note that these poems are not meant to insult anyone, but rather reflect my interpretation of our future: or what I envision for our future.

This is something I wrote when the Holy Spirit started to deepen its presence within me, allowing me to perceive God's purpose in everything.

MAN AND NATURE

I asked God to put people in my life without reason or conditions. Even though the seasons change, I'm still alive. I forgive myself for those things I've done, to myself and others.

The spark of the Holy Spirit is inside me now, and it's longing for a roaring flame to burst heavenly bound to an everlasting dream. This is soon to be our reality, too profound to be announced to those who don't believe.

But even though some can't understand, I know I must tell everyone I meet of His miraculous works, His words of wisdom, and how they've touched my heart and what it's doing for my soul. A new adventure, a new beginning, freedom from bondage, returning from a tormented life, made from bits and pieces of a tattered dream. I know God will never fail me, as long as I do what's put in front of me.

I love the wolves and what they represent, God's undying love for us and His creatures of this world, in which man shuns or destroys if it becomes a threat.

Most men don't understand what they are or what they live for. They live for each other, just like we should, to be free to do the cleanup and help the weak, so they don't have to suffer or stumble through life, to be with God and feel His loving touch.

What man does not understand, he destroys to suit his own needs. If it's a problem, dismantle it or tuck it away, so they don't have to deal with it. It's not just the wolves and the animals; it's the spirits in people who tolerate others at the cost of suffering and misguidance.

God forgives them to a point and uses us to show others His strength, that in numbers untold, we can free those who are bound to earth in self-gain. For God's wisdom and strength can flow stronger than anything imaginable that man could ever conceive. I see now what I truly need, and it's God and Jesus. God, I've always known, but I just didn't want to let go… and let Your Son walk with me. So at last, you have me, Lord God, do with me what you must. Show me what's expected of me, and I will, until the end, do Your gracious works.

These two poems are a reflection of reality. Open your mind and let them awaken your sense of hope, that we can change if we allow change!

NATURE'S THREAT, READY OR NOT

As I sit quietly amongst the misty trees, I wonder how life will turn out to be.

With all the feast, famine, death, and destruction, I can't see room for any reconstruction.

It hurts my heart to feel this way, that the world will crumble and fall someday.

The well-to-do are so wrapped up in endless acts, spending frivolously for the clothes on their backs.

They care not for others who are starving and trying to stay alive, that the general population is beginning to rise.

If everyone stopped just once to help someone, we could put some faith and hope back into humanity, then people just might reach for God, feeling His awesome power restoring their sanity.

Helping others and thoughts of good are two things that bring my memories back to the woods.

I wonder what nature thinks of us; very little, fear, or mistrust?

Maybe one day, when the moon is red, nature's creatures can lay safe in their beds.

Now, no one can say how life will turn out; once more, all I can do is shout and expound the pain that I feel, to those who have nothing, and to them, nothing is real.

NO FUTURE WITHOUT HOPE

The world population has focused readily on things that will be their end, they forgot all about God, who just wants to be their friend.

We multiply and reproduce, we pillage the world at large, we dump, and we dump toxic waste with a continuous steel barge.

We see barren lands that were once filled with breathing trees, and now they're raping the oceans, that were once beautiful blue seas!

God sees this ghastly scene and watches from afar, he knows that once we've tapped the resources here, we'll reach out for the stars.

When this happens, he will step in and clean house like no one has ever seen; he will choose those who will go or stay, according to the ones that hold their faith and pray each day.

Many will be mad at this choice and become prey for those who will give up, and darkness will settle in their hearts; for they never really believed from the very start.

All I can say is, hold on no matter what God may do, because the longer we endure our trials and sufferings, the more God's love will build inside of you!

For when it comes time to go, and he calls out with his warm soft voice, telling you it's time, we'll know it's peace that we feel, because we know we paid the price standing our ground, as we remained steadfast and still.

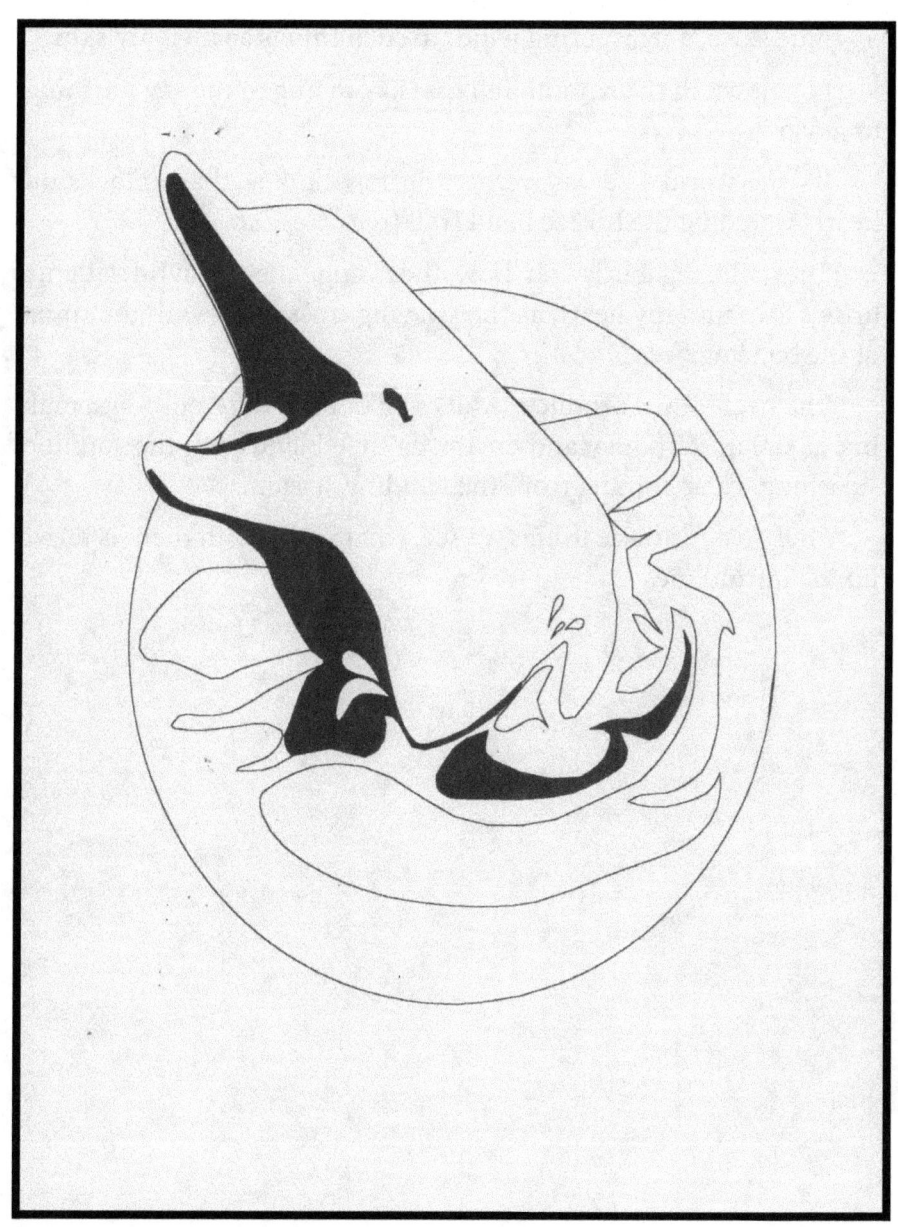

NATURE'S WAY

Blue skies, a whispering wind, to such things against my skin.

I lie down in the smooth tall grass, reaching to the sky for things to grasp.

It's the world I see as we beckon for the key, that unlocks our hearts watching the breeze bend frail trees.

The chirping birds, oh how they sing, their playful laughter brings love into my heart, as the swaying trees mesh with the sound of the buzzing bees.

The nectar they produce seduces all of us in different ways, making us dream of honey and cream, as they blend with the sound of splashing water coming from the winding stream.

God gives us these things we see; what we do with them is purely up to you and me.

MAMMALS: OUR FRIENDS?

Since the dawn of man mammals have saved and guided us in times of need. All they wanted was to be our friend and help us to learn about the sea.

If we could truly understand what they're saying when they speak, I truly believe they would say, "Let us be your friend, for we too are the meek and there is a message we send and we have what you seek."

The intelligence that they emit and what they're trying to convey, we should submit to God and the truth of His ways.

I really think God has linked them to man, to be there for us when we've been lost in that vast liquid sand.

The ocean mammals know of our veracious demands, and they continue to be our friends; no matter what we do, they still forgive us and remain true blue.

We need to learn this ourselves, to love one another no matter what, even when darkness dwells.

Think of the mammals; if we could put ourselves in their tight spot, we could learn how to forgive and put away what we've been taught.

If we weren't so obsessed with ourselves and pride, the jealousy of others would soon subside.

God has given us what we need to succeed, but some are unwilling to let the meek plant the seed.

What are you afraid of, is it weakness or love? We should love one another and put away self-gain and pride, for God and His Son want to truly be our friends, to teach us more about love and the true message they send.

FACE YOUR FEARS

Each day may seem small to some, but it's giant steps for me, for as in the past, I was a lonely man for all to see.

I now see God's purpose everywhere, as I shed my old ways, daring to be someone who really cares.

It has been a dream of mine to grow and be free, to show the true side of me, you see.

This is one that's been hidden behind fears of unseen sights, of dead-end hopes and endless frights.

Some may just laugh because they don't understand; they have no idea that they still carry their buckets of sand.

This weight so heavy on their minds, with unbelief, they're unwilling to be kind.

So to anyone who thinks they're fine or says, "Hey, look at me, I'm okay," has not the courage to say… "I'm scared, I'm weak, and I want to know God today."

CAN WE TRUST

My shattered life of twisted thoughts… measuring lengths untold, of broken dreams and muffled screams, of my life to others I've told.

I guess it's a lesson in life to learn, to trust once more again; we have to believe, or we won't really grow, with God's own words, this we know.

It can be dismal though if we hide in a hole, living in a world of mistrust; so we trust again and again to find a friend, and we end up back in our hole.

People wonder why we seem so shy and never give up our hearts at all; it's because our hearts are so fragile and deep, and we fear of having a fall.

I wonder now if I'll ever trust again, to let someone share my deepest thoughts or even be my friend?

There's nothing like having a friend, you see, these feelings held in a bond, but I'll keep searching and searching in those endless rings that seem to go nowhere in the pond.

A Tree, or a Big Stick with Leaves?

As life begins to unfold as we grow, we found the times when we learned how to be cold.

It comes from the environment in which we were raised. Our parents showed us how to live, so we were dazzled and dazed, because we knew no other way, our minds were completely amazed.

We look at them with that 100% trust, a mirror reflection like stainless steel, but on the other side, it's all covered with rust.

A tarnished life, passed on with pride. Somewhere along the line their souls were lost and wandered like the ocean tide.

It's a despair all its own, without a spark of life to be shown, no care or concern, or even a willingness to be known.

We hear of pride, we know how it's spelled, but I know for me, it always unlocked the many gates to hell.

It was always my demise, and a path well-known. I led others because this is what I've been told and shown.

Now if you have been taught that a tree is nothing but a big stick with leaves, let Jesus show you the difference, of what you see and what you perceive.

His love for you will change your mind. He will teach you love, and how to be kind.

It's a new world you see, and the barriers of pride, they will suddenly subside, if you just ask God to let his Son be your guide.

MAKING AMENDS

I used to be a person all used up inside, a man that would speak before thinking, not caring if others cried.

This I did out of habit from the many years of unjust insults and pent-up fears.

I confess to you Lord God, you see me when I favor the flesh. This mixes with my emotions, as they mesh together with your words like a spellbound potion driven by Satan's evil herd.

My intent when I speak tries to be words of concern, but my mouth becomes harsh because my tongue has not yet learned.

This is why we have amends, to humble ourselves before God and others, to confess to our sisters and brothers for what we said, that we can be wrong, and we shall lie in our own beds.

In time, this all shall pass when we train our reborn souls; to prepare for the time when we meet the Father and His Son, like others did on that grassy little knoll.

THEY POINT THE FINGER

When we come to know the Lord in a truthful way, there will be others who will point the finger and refute what you say.

It's jealousy from Satan that will always be a lie because they're still clinging to sin and they can't understand why. They struggle with the fact that clings to their back, with an ungodly truth that will sling rocks when they're attacked.

They want what you have, but they're unwilling to give way because the truth really hurts in what you have to say.

Satan's demons will cover your eyes, so you will always be pointing your finger like the blind man with fear and despise.

They say to themselves when they see someone else, "How come they have what I want, and I can't get peace within myself?"

Satan fools us with his clever little lies that we're okay, and we don't have to hate what we should despise.

As we still do these sinful deeds, love can't fill your heart, as we struggle to hold tight to our old ways that used to tear us apart.

Until we're able to see the real truth for what it is, we'll continue to point the finger. So listen to what you say, for Galatians Chapter Five will make you see three fingers pointing back your way.

STAND FOR FIGHT

When we feel like we're out of control, should we stand and fight, or hold precious to what belongs to God, this being our very soul.

We could stand and argue until no one wins, or let go of our will and choose not to sin.

Satan would rather have us stand and fight, breaking our bond with the Lord. He needs us to release vile hate and pain, using that double-edged sword.

Satan's world is filled with lust, greed, and crime. He's a sickly one with an earthly goal, searching for anyone, taking them down to his hellish hole.

I've learned to pray for many who stray, for those caught in the clutches of Satan's petty ways.

Satan, I choose not to lose as I toss you aside, just as I did with my foolish pride. And now I show others that God doesn't want us to run and hide.

I see you now, who you really are, and how you use others for play. God showed me a different way, and it makes it much easier to say, "Satan, be gone with you by the blood of Jesus Christ of Nazareth, and I cast from my life of shame. No longer can you make me feel that I have to take the blame."

For I now am a man of God, and I praise His name out loud. I ask God proudly to free the saints, the many still blinded by Satan's evil shroud.

GUIDE ME

When I open my eyes, I turn my will and my life to the Lord. I ask for His grace while I glimpse once more at a new morning sky, with a smile on my face, not with an outlook all gloomy, and I want to die!

I do this before I place my feet on the floor. I pray for strength and wisdom, like I did the day before.

My day begins, and I'm on my way, with God's graceful words flowing in everything I say.

I'm a simple man coming from a complicated life. It's a spontaneous life, and action is the key to His glorious works that are inside you and me.

Be it not for me to say what will happen today, for I know His will be done. I teach others what I know about His one and only Son.

God's love and protection flow freely in me as I continue to walk in His ways. They see God in my eyes as I calmly stroll by while I mingle in the world today.

I live by the truth, be it known, this I know by God's own words, to be the only truth today, the best truth I've ever heard.

Remove These Chains

Growing old but still tough and bold, I remember the times I was so cruel and cold.

To be pure at heart seemed distant to me, that I tried to scream because I just couldn't see.

I felt this choking weight around my neck; it gagged my life and it felt like heavy chains. For the years were my pains and the pains were my fears, there was a need and a longing for my pent-up tears.

Every day I work with the Lord to remove these bonds, this bounding metal mass that holds back my future and clings to my past.

I dream one day I'll be completely set free; this is when God will take me home, to stand before Him and Jesus in the kingdom of heaven, to be recognized and known.

The dream is real, and I know it to be true. I'm not alone anymore because I know God is there, I know I can feel Him… can't you?

PRAY, OBEY, BE AMAZED

I'm learning new things as I pray each day, new meanings, new thoughts. I'm so amazed I have a new mind today.

More and more as the miracles occur, I see them so clear as I let Jesus cleanse me and I work towards being pure.

Pure at heart was a new beginning for me, I let others know of how the Holy Spirit has allowed me to see.

The darkness that lurks in the unbelievers' hearts, they lash out with their evil tongues that can cause our serenity to depart.

With God's strength, I can stand my ground. I pray for many as I sense Satan's demons scurrying and running around.

I lack judgment sometimes as the flesh returns, I try to obey as I gather my strength and apply what I've learned.

Satan is trying to do battle with me on Holy ground, but as long as I stay in the circle, I will win the battle for my crown.

For I am a winner today, not the loser that I was, this is what I was taught, that a loser always does.

A loser always lashes out when their luck runs dry, we attack our friends for they must be secretly laughing as we wallowed and cried.

When we're lost and we run on self-will, our minds are about to explode, and our hearts are like a cold winter's chill.

This is what happens when we know no other way, but there is a new life, if we reach out and pray. Along with prayer comes the willingness to obey, to follow God's commands, and hear what the Holy Spirit has to say.

So when we practice these simple rules that are so easy and set, we will surely be amazed with the warmth of our hearts, and the gifts we'll get.

WAITING FOR GOD'S CHOICE

I'm looking for love in which intimacy is found, a joining of two souls who are striving towards a heavenly crown.

I need someone in my life to share my love, to fill that special place in my heart that I've set aside from the decision above.

God showed me her caring smile that can do no wrong. I can feel her heart, its rhythm is so smooth, it beats so strong.

All darkness can be removed by her compassionate touch; I can tell you this much, she lives by God's will, and I shall wait, remaining steadfast and still.

She has love for all she meets, her eyes can warm many hearts and her actions are so petite.

I've longed for the day to meet this woman that God has chosen, the woman of my dreams, that perfect rose.

I know she can unlock my gentle love, this love that has been a secret behind a lost and bitter soul, waiting for the time we're joined, and my life becomes whole.

Once I feel her touch, my senses will ignite that flame, I've been waiting anxiously, I miss her so much.

I know she's out there, but where, I don't know. As long as I continue in God's word, he'll take me where I need to go.

WHAT WE GAIN WITH PRAISE

Never before have I thought this way, to speak of God's words and give Him praise.

I can't take credit for anything that I do, for God is always there, and He gives me strength to ensue.

More and more God keeps His word, I tell others of what I've heard.

As long as I expound in praise for all to hear, I grow in spirit and there's nothing that I fear.

I used to be afraid of everything in my way, but now I know I was afraid to pray.

I see now what I couldn't see before, the little child inside that was afraid of that door.

The door that would open if I were willing to knock, the door I felt that would never unlock.

I've had a fear of locked doors all my life, but God handed me the key as He heard my plea and said, "Come in, my Son, and I'll show you what you've missed in Me."

Well, praise to God, He showed me His ways; He showed me His power and His awesome power of praise.

SO WHAT NOW?

I see birds, I see laughter, I see time, I hear words, does that sound selfish, or too unreal to be heard?

You hear my prayers, Lord, you know my thoughts, you know my wants, you know my needs, but all that you've given me, I fear I won't succeed.

You've shown me my life and how I've battered my dreams, you've given me the gift to interpret when others scheme.

You've given me the speech of love and compassion in so many ways, I write them in poems and I will expound them throughout the days.

You've blessed my heart and you're still cleaning my mind, you say in your words, I must forgive and be kind.

You've shown me love, you revealed life to me, now I see the world, and the way it's supposed to be.

Life is a process, a refining mode, to become your humble servant, to bear your many loads. This is why you gave me a strong heart, a strong mind, and a strong back as you pound away and refine.

You know I'm impatient and how I can be, yet you still hold true because you believe in me.

But my old thoughts are still stuck to my back, like a monkey riding a dog, using a whip with an endless attack.

Those painstaking thoughts that kept me bound and chained, I think to myself in a selfish way, "what now Lord, I've endured so many many days?"

My negative thoughts begin to outweigh my good, as I look in the mirror saying, "you're a loser and you'll amount to no good, you're turning out to be just like everyone said you would."

At times, it's hard not to think these useless words I say, like, "what's the use, I might as well give up today."

But you don't let me give in, you encourage me to humble myself before another, a brother in Christ, that will help me blow my cover.

The blanket of fear pulled tight over my head, that blinds my eyes from your words you've said.

You've told me so often in the Bible, and also in rhymes, that you'll always be true, so many many times.

So, another lesson to be learned and a repentance to be made, a return from darkness and enter the light, you once again give me the courage to stand tall, and hold on with all my might.

Receiving the Seed

Since I accepted the Lord and His Son into my life, I've grown each day, putting to rest my troubles and strife.

There's a wish today and a hope inside, of many feelings lost and lies I've told, but now God has given me life and to God my life I've sold.

It was just a wish then, now I hold it dear to my heart, as I pray for others to find a start.

For now, I am a kind man, coming from a strange and desolate land. I long for the time when I meet God and His Son, and walk by their side when the rapture is done.

Until we accept the Lord and His Son into our lives, we will remain in our own hell, looking for the answers to release us from our hardened shell.

We can't see His miracles which are happening all around us because we're too busy being misguided and stuffing our trust.

Some ask themselves, "why, why, why me? As they begin to cry." What is it? A loss of pride, a loss of another gone, lonely? What is it we can't see? Maybe that's when God wants you all for Himself… Hmm, could this be?

If we could all slow down just long enough and trust in God's word, we could see His purpose everywhere, finding what we need. Then we can plant more thoughts while growing His glorious seed.

This seed will soon sprout into one of God's children, showing others a new life untold, and even to them God's doors will open, and His arms will reach out and unfold.

Just remember, to forgive is divine and speak words from your heart with nothing attached, for the rewards will come like an endless rhyme. This will only happen if we receive the seed and plant it in time.

GOD'S TALK

Before when I spoke, my words were nothing but an alphabet, a babbling joke.

When I received the Holy Spirit, I asked God for His words to flow free, I felt His authority and His glorious transformation growing inside of me.

As I listened to the words that made every ear bend, I tingled as I heard the message that You send.

It seems the only ones who know what I mean are the ones who have accepted Jesus and have submitted their lives to coming clean.

To others, they know and hear what I say, "pray for forgiveness from your heart, and Jesus will start a warming blaze from a solid little spark."

To know the feelings I get and the outcome when I pray, makes all the difference in what I say today.

I don't reach for a message for others to hear; for when I speak, it's God's words bringing faith, hope, and cheer.

RIDING THE LINE

When we've been down that darkened path in which we were lost in sin, we stumbled and fell in front of God and staggered to His door, wondering if He'd even let us in.

The golden door that glistened so, it opened wide to let us in; we listened to the promises given by God's own word, "we should confess our wrongs and praise His name with worship and song."

We should also confess to another of our faults and our walk will soon commence, just stay in step and don't walk the line, for God is there just on the other side of the fence.

Well now that our minds are at ease and thinking we've done our best, can we give our hearts to God and trust that He'll do the rest?

We pondered to ourselves, our feet still stuck in the door, we look back at darkness wondering if we can go back there once more.

We ride the line balancing our souls, carrying our mixed up thoughts that kept us from being whole.

Now you can ride the line of good and bad, but God sees this in time, He's waiting for you while feeling sad. For God needs you to take a break, and cry out to His one and only Son, who is not a fake.

You see, God is a grandstander and has patience beyond belief, He loves you no matter what, be it a murderer or a thief.

He doesn't trick you or set you up; He lets you decide if you want to suit up!

GREAT EXPECTATIONS

When I was young, I was taught the ways of the truth. They said the truth was better than a lie. If I told the truth, I would get in less trouble and the belt wouldn't make me cry.

So my expectations of the truth were soon filled with lies because the belt was still there to bring tears to my eyes.

This was the beginning of an untrustworthy life, of trusting many and expecting strife.

For whenever I asked for a favor returned, I'd get a "sure," a wave, or a convincing smile. But when it came time, I knew too well that the smile was fake and my anger would swell.

Time after time, I expected more and more. It drove me wild as I stomped my feet on the floor.

I would always think, "How could they treat me this way? They said they would be there for me on this day."

I would never go back on my word. How dare they make me act this way? I was trustworthy and would always do what I say!

Oh yes, in my mind, I was truly a saint. But I forgot all the times I had let others down, and their lives I surely did taint.

The circle of life that goes round and round, it comes back to you; then it lets you down!

Because this is the rule for which all truth stands, for each negative reaction, there are unrealistic demands.

The demands that we expect others to obey, the ones we expect to be done today.

Then there are the "Great Expectations" we put on ourselves, the ones so high up out of our reach, there isn't a ladder tall enough for these shelves.

This would always end up with our minds set ablaze, and people would be burdened with our unrealistic daze.

They would see us shout and wave our arms, to see us rave as we showed them our childish charms.

Until one day when we've surely had enough, we would turn to the people that could open our eyes. They would show us about true love and guide our souls to our Lord in the skies.

This will come when you're willing to receive the splendor of life and the true meaning of the seed.

So many people hold onto their rights, to stand alone, to put up a good fight.

Let me tell you, people, there is only one who can break those chains that bound our thoughts to unrealistic gain, that one is God. He'll always remain and help you through your troubled pain.

There are the Great Expectations of life that we should never put on ourselves or anyone else, for this can be done if you're willing to get out of yourself.

You see, it boils down to this: if we never expect someone to always come through and never set the stage, there can be no reason to raise our hands to another and shout in a fuming rage.

GAMES PEOPLE PLAY

Children are not responsible for their childish acts, but adults do it out of envy, spite, or jealousy, this is a cold hard fact.

They're so wrapped up in their old cold ways, that they act like children, except children have an excuse to play.

Children are young, they haven't learned what it means to act out in revenge, but adults do. This happens when they see others happy and free because their lives are so miserable, they would do anything to get at you and me.

What a hopeless way to live, so unbalanced, hanging onto that dark side, that jealousy, that envy, that foolish pride!

I look back on how my life used to be, I did many dark things, the reason; I just couldn't see.

I couldn't understand why I acted out with malice in a childlike way. It was hard for me to comprehend, so now I kneel and pray.

Acting like a child with blinding fists of hate, can lead you down so fast to Satan's rusty gate!

God wants us to become children again, to feel the freedom we once had when we were so innocent, just a young little lass or lad.

Do something for God; look in the mirror and tell me what you see. If you see a twisted, disfigured face look up at God and ask him, "Is this what you want me to be?"

If you're not broken, and you answer yourself yes, that's what you'll become: a heartless, worn-out soul, and a burden to some. You will continue to stumble and fall while Satan has his way. The sad part is, you don't even know he's there, because he's so subtle while leading you astray.

You will wander endlessly as Satan beats you within an inch of your life; that inch is Satan's mile that makes you frown and unable to smile.

So quit playing those games with that evil word, despise, for it will eventually break you down and cover your lonely eyes.

God wants you to know what it's like to feel his healing hands, and let me tell you, he won't take the blame for your lonely guilt or your childish demands.

He's waiting patiently, with open arms, extending his warm, soothing hands. He's a caring God, with love for all, and to all he understands.

LEARNING

What I learned today will help me grow, to live each day to hear the rooster crow.

Feelings unknown, to others I've shown, the true meaning of change and how I've grown.

It's a seed, you see, that's been planted in me, to feed my soul when I encased in a bowl.

I want to live and be free once more, to shed my old ways and settle the score.

I look forward now and I stay in step, and remind myself to never forget.

My pain has been deep and the cut was wide, but what does it take to learn and just drop my pride?

I see life now and how it's supposed to be, God prepares my path as I learn His ways. Now I give God all the glory and praise, as my life gets better day by day.

VIOLENCE OR BLINDNESS

There are times when we're so quick to strike out with a vicious blow, that we don't know why we did it, or was it just for show?

Some people were raised to be bold, to stand your ground, stand tall they were told.

These words have been passed down from generation to generation, from Father to son, to hold your ground and never run.

God doesn't tell these awful lies, he says, "repent, give up your evil ways and violence, or soon His wrath will come upon you in future days."

I have lived with violence all my life, in my heart and in my mind, but I knew no better because I was taught that being kind was weak and for weakness there was no time.

I have found that a man is nothing without love, love for all, even for those who act stern and stand with their backs to the wall.

When someone lashes out in a sinful way, we let God do His works and in our minds we pray.

It isn't for us to understand or reason why, but to lend a hand as we breathe deep and let go with a peaceful inner sigh.

We pray for forgiveness because they know no other way, this is what they've been shown, by the many who stray.

They're unwilling to conceive life on God's own terms, so they continue on and on because they're reluctant to learn.

It's so simple, it's easy to be kind, but some would rather create more energy to be bold and blind. Just think of it, the time we waste on violent thoughts, the energy expended on physical threats, that we think of later with deep regrets.

But do we turn our heads away in shame? No, because in our minds they were the ones to blame. We should stop when violence begins to rise, then ask God what He would do; I know I would hear His voice when someone has done me wrong, He would say this, "ask for my strength and I'll give you my hand and I'll show you what it's like to walk away and be a real man."

What God has intended for all mankind, is to be helpful, gracious, and caring towards the blind.

There are many who deep in their hearts would give anything to be kind, but they can't turn away, because they've been taught down through the ages, by the many that were so bold and blind.

I AM BUT A STONE

Life begins when you start all over, pulling off the sheets and blowing your own cover.

There's a sense that the real me can't hide, the spirit of life that's me inside.

Life enters my soul and soon begins to fill that deep empty hole, because it's time for me to surrender and play a new role.

I'm like a rock, my exterior is so tough and coarse, but my shell can be broken in the blink of an eye, while the inside stays solid and unable to cry.

As people try to crack my exterior and hammer away, I think to myself, "Are these people for real what they say? Am I too harsh and I need to pray?"

Oh yes, they're right and I shall surrender gladly without a fight.

So let them chip away at my pride and show me how to change, because now my life has meaning and a much broader range.

Then suddenly it happened, instead of taking a stand, I look them straight in the eye and offer them my hand.

It's a tough one to do, make no mistake, but being genuine is real and the handshake is no fake.

When the Holy Spirit has entered our bodies, it's a feeling like no other, it makes you see and feel like everyone is your sister or brother. The thoughts of ill feelings fade slowly away, like a soft cool mist that will lift in time and soon turn into a beautiful day.

OVER AND OVER

When we are unbelievers and caught in sin, we always wonder: why can't we move forward and win?

This is the question that has plagued many women and men, why is there no end and where do I begin?

Most often we're subject to our own demise, that we can't see the answer that has been right in front of our eyes.

Take for example someone who abuses alcohol, drugs, or sex. Their minds are cluttered with lies, so everything seems complex.

This is the truth that finally came to me, that I was the reason that I couldn't really feel free.

For I hadn't let go of the sickening pain, the things God only knew that I did over and over again.

Now the answers lie deep in your heart and the recesses of your mind. Do you want to do it over and over and live like you're blind, or will you let God be your guide, so you may move forward and the tangled mess unwind?

SILENCE IS GOLDEN

As I grow in silence, I hear these golden words, these many thoughts of silent prayers coming from those I've heard.

I pray each day as I grow inside, praying for knowledge and will, I receive more and more as the days go on, to my heart this surely does fill.

I think of those who struggle and fight, trying to gain a foothold in the roads of life.

They grasp at anything near to them they can, they hold tight, asking for God's strength and the will to endure the temptations of the night.

I can't describe the bliss that I feel, for I am a man of concern; I search my mind filled with God's holy words, with these I really can learn.

As I open my heart, unfolding my arms, I reach out to many with true love, feelings, and charms.

I feel God's love growing steadily each day; He nurtures the seed, and I thank Him for His love as I humbly bow before Him on my knees.

God continues to say, "Read, read, read my words, just walk towards me, and your prayers will surely be heard."

I Can Feel Love Now

My eyes see much clearer now; before shadow people filled my life. That life was filled with many dark clouds, and now, with God in my life, I no longer have to ask the questions of how and why.

There's a feeling today when I think of all the good I can do, the thoughts, the hopes, the feelings for you.

My senses are alive with tingling thoughts of little puppy dogs, teddy bears, and tiny little tots.

These are most precious indeed, to hold in our caring arms; to show them by our faith and let them know they're safe from any harm.

It's a fire that's grown, its flame emits warmth and strength. It holds us together and all in place; it's God's undying love, feelings, and grace.

FIRST GIFT OF CHRISTMAS

Since the days of the Lord, His prophets talked of hope and deliverance from a King like no other, that would not look down on anyone and would treat them as though they were a loving sister or brother.

While the world grew, the Lord demanded many things from them, and one that He wanted the most was their undying love. If given, the Lord would grant them the desires of their heart that could only come from the heavens above.

The only thing they had to do was make a commitment to a God they could not see. They knew He was real because those before them spoke with the Lord and they truly believed.

But as time went on, many strayed and the sin in man grew, and Satan filled their hearts with wicked desires and their own lust they did ensure.

So one day, the Lord was ready to meet them face to face, but He could not do this in His godly form, for their hearts would melt from their unbelief and disgrace.

The coming was near, and Satan feeling like he was god, but God would not kill all the firstborn, but once again, His lies had missed one, that soon many would adorn.

On a night so clear, it seemed like the stars were angels, and the chosen felt honored as they knelt in His presence, while the Lord cried at His birth and He filled their eyes with joyful tears, revering the Lord with self-worth.

Time went on, moving from place to place, showing mercy and grace, as He demonstrated to many that He was not only God but His only Son in His place.

Now stop for a moment and think of His birth. It was not celebrated with showers of gifts and presents for all, but prayers to the

Lord and not spending all their time shopping in the mall.

Now, some may have forgotten the first gift of Christmas ever given to mankind, an everlasting presence of Jesus that would remind ourselves to be faithful and kind.

So the next time Christmas rolls around and the hustle and bustle makes you angry while standing in line, try putting away your money and think of Jesus, how He died on the cross after healing the sick and gave sight to the man who was born blind.

THINK BEFORE YOU SPEAK

Please be careful and choose your words, because people can be so cruel to the point of being absurd.

I see every day how people's sadness is openly displayed, where they make their point as they become blinded and dismayed.

They see their lives fading slowly away, so their tongues will lash out while their days are numbered, and we continue to pray.

So please remember and be kind, because Christians are not stupid and definitely not blind.

From Madness to Jesus

These next few poems are about drugs and alcohol and the effects they have on our lives and our souls.

Too Tough

There comes a time in life to live or die, or continue to be a prisoner to our addictions that will always be a lie.

They strip our pride, they remove all feelings as they take us for a most ghastly ride.

Our mind and body being sound and true, can't conceive life like we used to do.

With our minds full of alcohol and our crazy ways of life, we are soon filled with nightmares that will eventually take our lives.

We believe it will be the same, but we know it's really not, when our bodies get tired and sluggish because we can't get what we need, and soon our stomachs are tied in deep, helpless knots.

We become ruthless and vile, lying in gutters shivering and choking on our own bile.

Now, if we are fortunate enough to still have a home, we call to God once more as we hug the porcelain base, lying on the floor with our face in disgrace.

We swear it would be the last, if God would help us through it; God did what He promised, but we forget Him again, as we lay in our own vulgar mess and once again we sin.

When the pain becomes too much, we have thoughts of deep despair, because our minds are warped and sizzled and we think there's no one who cares.

When we've had enough, we find weakness is our strength. God lets us know He's there when He hears our cries, as He flashes our lives before our lonely eyes.

We had no idea our lives would end up like this, lying in the gutter with our mouth open wide, spewing the foul odor of our muttering pride.

Suddenly we shout to ourselves as we get up off the ground,

throwing down the bottle, and we end up falling down.

Weak and desperate, we look up in the sky, asking God once more to save us, with tears beginning in our eyes.

With our arms stretched out wide, we shed rivers of lonely years. We begin to build back our pride and shed more and more tears.

With barely the strength to crawl, God guides us home. He lets you decide who to call, a friend or family, to ask them for help to stand tall.

Now the ways are surely not that easy and the road is really rough… but how much do you want to change your life… Is it really that hard… or are you just too tough?

NO LOVE IN THE BOTTLE, JUST THE WALKING DEAD

I looked for love in so many places, I searched for compassion in many, many faces.

No one had compassion for me, I was a lonely man for all to see.

I expected sympathy from all who heard, a simple smile, a subtle word.

They saw my laughter, they saw my wit, but behind the smile, my pain did sit.

It was a longing for love and my pain ran deep, and alcohol was my love. So into a bottle I would creep.

It made me feel like I belonged and I felt no pain, but the ultimate end was always the same: false laughter, endless dreams, endless searching, and maddening screams.

The screams were certainly not of joy, there was no fun for this grown-up boy.

I would wake each morning with my head split wide, rubbing my stomach, for it was empty inside.

I searched for my heart and I could feel a beat, but it pumped only blood alcohol and my love for the bottle was the only thing I could eat.

There wasn't a day that passed by on my quest for love, there were very few takers I could speak highly of.

The ones that were kind and right for me, I tossed them aside as I ran to my love and into a bottle I would hide.

I know what it was, their love didn't seem real, I was so blind and unable to feel, because to me love served no purpose and the bottle promised me an endless seal. It would never let me down and it would always be there, as long as I had money, it would keep me in its care.

But time went on and my life grew dim, looking through a bottle and living on a whim.

The days grew shorter as I slept in a haze, only to come to with my eyes all blurry and glazed.

Feeling like the world had left me behind, I would reach into my pocket and find nothing but a dime.

Broke once again and the sickness so strong, I would rage to myself and try to figure out what went wrong.

For the night before, I said with a cheer, "I'll go home early tonight and get up with the dawn, I'll get out of town and go where the salmon spawn."

Once again, a shattered dream and nothing but a dime to head towards the stream.

I watched my life fade slowly away, working my way towards the street, day by day.

It didn't take long before I had lost it all, my friends, my family, and my pride that used to help me stand tall.

Well, the walls were built and its face was high, I wallowed in self-pity thinking, "poor me, poor me" as I cried.

Back and forth from the bar to the curb, my life in shambles and my mind absurd.

I beat myself down as I relived my past, I saw my life going nowhere and it was falling fast.

I saw twenty years of nothing to show, but empty bottles all lined up in a row.

This obsession for the bottle distorted everything I knew, it had to be put to rest and I knew what to do!

Even though I had tried many times before, I had to take a stand and humbly ask God to open His heavenly doors.

I really meant what I said when I asked God to restore my mind and clear my head, because it was time to live, and return from the walking dead!

MY EARTHY GUIDE

When we finally accept surrender and we've fallen flat on our face, we look up to see a hand, It's our earthly defender seeing us lay in disgrace.

It's someone who's been right where you are, one who's learned to heal many many scars.

Through years of practice helping others how to stand, he reaches out to you with a helping hand.

Even though we may not like what we hear, we have made a choice, it was better than drinking beer.

At least in the morning we can remember what we said and the night before, it's so clear in our heads and we want to know more.

This is not the end, this is only the beginning of the message that he sends.

For we have a shell that's been hardened by hell, this will take time to crack, for we have lots to tell.

Our guide listens as we expound our rage, for those who have hurt us and kept us bound and caged.

Oh yes, everyone else is to blame, why should we take the fall, we had no part in this at all.

Oh contraire mon ami, this was your fault and you soon shall see.

Our guide begins to teach us how to walk, to hold our head up high, to see the many colors as we look up towards the sky.

As we open our ears and listen to his words, things become more clear, as we marvel at the sounds of the singing birds. What we've missed with our heads full of beer, those things we never saw before and now we hold them oh so dear.

Now that our guide has taught us how to live, it is time to learn what it's like to give.

For God gives freely and says, "Do not doubt", suddenly you feel His presence, then you know what clarity is all about.

God has given you peace, a jump start on your heart, you feel it beat with a rhythm so strong, you feel the sorrow for those things you've done wrong.

What is this, tears of joy; this is a miracle for this grown-up boy!

For many years we've deprived ourselves the right to really live, now we've found true joy and God tells us we must forgive.

Forgive others and soon you'll see the difference it makes when God cleans your mind and sets you free!

It's a feeling a prisoner can only understand, the one who has been trapped with a beer glued to their hand.

Who could better tell this story all too well, of the return from a nightmare; a nightmare of an alcoholic hell!

A WHITE DEAD END

Most of us in life, when we begin, don't know where we're going or where we've been.

We see people all around us, happy and having fun, where once they were weak and desperate, seeking recognition on the run.

Now they seem content because they feel like they belong, this newfound friend has really made them strong.

It seemed a person approached them and assured a change in their life would occur, he pulled something from his pocket and said, "This is the cure."

Well, he didn't steer them wrong, the hope he had promised them was there, the problem was evident, he didn't really care.

It gave them courage beyond imagination, letting their minds run free, but little did they know there was a clause and an end to this wild spree.

Utopia, what a farce, a dull sense of white hope, I don't think so, why do you think they call it dope?

Of course, someone always tries to explain what will happen in the end, but no one will believe, then it's too late and you see there's no way you can leave.

Now, many can attest to the damage and wreckage in their lives, that started from a small white package and a glistening in their eyes.

It gave them false thrills and spine-tingling chills, from the sparkling white death of false hope.

It has no vice, no guilt, no conscience, it will be your best friend, it will even make you unable to cope and it will still be there until your end.

This white death will eventually make you hate and do everything you despise.

Accept this fact and begin to run, because in the end, there won't be any room for fun.

It's no way to live and a one-way street, don't think you'll win because you're already beat.

If you decide and want to live, don't stop to say hello, because the patience of white death is insurmountable on the run.

It will pat you on the back telling you a job well done, all the while sizing you up for the very next run.

Be careful, make no mistake, take charge of your life, because white death doesn't make any mistakes when it comes to taking your life.

White death challenges you over and over again, and when everything you've ever hoped for is gone; when this happens, and believe me it will, white death will have you right where it wants, and you will think everyone's to blame.

It will leave you heartless and cruel, for this is its rule, and ultimately leaves you lonely and dying in shame!

Now, if you can't relate to this, keep playing with white death, and it will show you to the gates of Hell!

SOMETHING THEY SAID

Many times before, I've tried to show a true desire to shake my sinful side. I wanted so much to change, but I was unwilling to learn. I was so deranged.

I asked for help with a motive in mind: just help me get on track and help me out of my bind.

Well, they watched me as I did my dance, then they told me the truth, and I gave them the evil glance.

How dare they say these things so true? Don't they know I have pride? How would you like it if I did that to you?

Poor me, poor me, poor me, another drink. How dare they tell me how to think!

They knew me all too well because they had been there too, that evil place where Satan dwells.

I couldn't understand, I just couldn't confess that my life was in shambles and my mind was a mess.

Well, I tried, and I tried, and I kept coming back because I saw something they had, something my life had lacked.

It took many fits of rage to unlock my cage, but soon I found the key, the key to my rage!

I found the key lost deep in my pride, the fear of loneliness that made me humble as I cried.

It came when I had tossed the last inch of my rope. The only thing that was left was to ask God if there was still any hope.

Well, He showed me His love that had never been lost. It was all my doing, and I held onto it at any cost.

But that cost was my life. It was fading fast, a pine box to fit into an earthly cast. God felt it was time to show me His hand, to lead me out of darkness and show me how to stand.

He made me realize what they said was true, but that Satan had a hand in this one too!

I've been a puppet on a mess of strings that tangled my life and strangled my dreams.

"Oh Satan, you were good, but God showed me that I'm not made of wood. No longer can you pull my strings, for the belt of truth surely does ring!"

It sings so loud with a pitch that drives you wild, and I tell you this: you no longer have your hands on this lost little child!

Praise be to God who has shown me His ways, and I'm very proud to say: "I love you God for saving my life, and I now show my gratitude as I kneel and pray."

RELAPSE

Relapse takes on many forms. This we can't afford, but sometimes it's an inevitable part of life for us to really understand the true meaning of the effects it has on our sanity and others around us.

Our actions while under the influence of any alcohol or drugs warrant the intervention of someone besides ourselves because we, as mere human beings, can only think of one thing: what satisfies our flesh. There is no amount of money, no single person that can relieve our pain and anguish from worldly sin except God, and only through His Son can we receive His love and help.

I've seen the darkness in many forms. Some are very subtle, and many are possessed by spirits that are unrecognizable. They keep us wrapped tightly in a blanket of hate; all they see is what the spirit tells them to see.

There are many Christians who still can't understand that the things they don't like in others are controlled by the prince of this world, and Satan gets his enjoyment out of people who can't understand loving others no matter what, but hate the sin that compels our actions and emotions. I, for one, still have a hard time when I see and feel the hate in others, but as long as I stay in the word of our Lord and Jesus Christ, I am constantly reminded: "Love thy Lord your God with all your heart and soul and with all your mind and with all your strength." The second is, "Love thy neighbor as yourself." There are no commandments greater than these.

If we can stop and think of these two powerful thoughts, Jesus will step in and let us feel love instead of hate, not saying we wouldn't feel anguish because we all have feelings, but Jesus would be there to stop us from doing wrong, just as long as we listen. I will never say that I am perfect because I won't be until God takes me home, and then and only then will I be complete. It's hard living for God because so many are against what He represents. This is because they don't understand; they only retain what matters to them, running their own lives. I tried running my own life again, and guess what? No matter what I did, no matter what I thought, my life was still incomplete. You see, when you take God out of the picture, Satan is there with all his temptations and lies, and in the end, he will consume you and your soul and take you with him into the pits of hell, along with all the rest of the individuals who thought they could do it all by themselves.

There is no true love without God and Jesus. I am living proof of that. Without keeping that continuous conscious contact on a daily basis, Satan will always be there to torment us with people whom he controls. Satan can only control what we give him, and if we give him enough room to squeeze through our doors, he will open the doors to our past and ridicule us with guilt and shame, keeping us in constant turmoil.

Once we come to know Jesus, Satan can't stand it, and he will do whatever it takes to get us back. This includes taking away something we idolize, be it a house, personal items, our family members, our jobs, etc. He will do anything to keep our minds on self-will instead of accepting that it's God's will that strengthens us. Only through humility can we ask for God's mercy and grace, and only then may we be able to stand in the fire with true faith, standing for God, no matter what.

FRIENDS

Inside us all, we feel the hurt as we act so straight and stern. People smile as they wave their hand, but is that mask meant just for me, as you use your palm as a fan?

Can we look inside for the things we hide while masking the real thoughts we have?

Some people can put on a front while they look you straight in the eye, then when you leave, their tongue becomes full of deceit and lies.

But in the end, they'll lose this friend and they'll wonder why, searching around every corner and bend.

It's just a matter of time until they burn this friend. There's a limit to how far they will go. There was a time when they held you on high, now God says, say hello and goodbye.

You may think this person has turned on you, but they have you deep in prayer. God knows of your pain; His ear is bent with patience, love, and care.

So, you can walk around with that scornful look in your eyes or learn from your Brother as you release your pride, letting go of all that guilt and shame with excuses for the many reasons why.

So remember, if friendship means nothing to you and you have no friends at all, just remember when you had a friend, and in their eyes, you once were standing tall.

ACCEPTANCE

There are things to accept that may seem inept; they can soon make us forget why we're here. We can roll with the punch when we seem out to lunch, or continue running in the dark and living on a hunch.

Now, at last, I'm not haunted by my past. I will accept those things that seem like dreams, and all I have to do is look to God and ask.

Though it may seem strange to some and a wavering thought, only God knows the outcome, and my soul He surely has caught.

A NEW PATH

Strolling down memory lane, I'm searching for answers and resolutions to gain.

I see where my path has led me this time, to learn how to love, and that's not a crime!

Willingness and honesty can make me forgive, because time is so precious, and I want so much to live!

Most of my life, I've been a prisoner to my addictions. They seemed like heavy chains. I've ridden the wild horse, and now I've retrieved the reins.

Be it not for me to say what will happen in my future days, all I can do is trust in God before it takes me to an early grave.

IT'S JUST GROWTH

Today, there seems to be a knot, a basketball-sized knot in a peculiar spot.

It's a nauseating pain that tugs at every nerve and vein; it's something unsure for my mind to ponder, for those wayward thoughts that kept me bound and made me wander.

I really don't like feeling this way, but I guess it's just growth, I have to say.

I have a need to be normal, not just walk the line, to cope with my inner self and not just do the time.

It's my past sins that remind me of the tide that moves slowly in, then in time, it moves slowly out. This is when I raise my eyes to God, asking for strength. "Lord, I gave you my life, and I lift my hands, I applaud at your power like a drummer in a band."

God knows I'm looking for that inner peace, a forgiveness that I can hold and see. My soul is expanding towards the sky, and I feel His love as He soothes me when I cry.

Now, I thank you God, for showing me mercy for my sins, and now I will continue to live, for my life is just growth for everyone to see, for my life is a miracle meant just for me.

I May Be Poor, but I Am Rich

Some say that money is the root of all evil, but to others, they say it's a farce; because to them: money is their friend and a giver of those worldly things, but really, it's only sadness and fame, so who's to blame for these terrible things that money brings.

There once was a time that God was in most people's hearts. This feeling has been missed and blown all apart.

Now, it's a race for the mighty buck, to see who can gain the most before the lightning has struck.

God watches these people devour others' pride, to take from the poor and take them for a ride.

When the time comes, and believe me it will, there will be nowhere to hide, not even inside a hill.

I love the gifts God has given me, especially the one to truly see. I've sat back for so many years, gagging on my tears, watching the world slowly fall. So many starving, so many getting rich, saving for the time that God throws the switch.

I'm smiling right now as I write this poem, for I know one day I'll be going home.

I will have a restful peace in my heart, knowing none of this was my demise, for the people who felt the pain and suffering that I saw in their sorrowful eyes.

God wants us to give generously to others who are in need, to simply steer away from lust and greed.

Lust for money, lust for power, don't be foolish and wait until the final hour.

For when the time comes, they'll rush in like mad dogs, lifting their hands in the air, screaming at God to forgive them of their sins, with evil in their hearts and a wild stare.

God will tell them, "You had your chance, I showed you the way to heaven's gate, but you showed no fear and shut your doors, and now I tell you it's too late!"

"Your time is up, and you should have known as you flipped your nose in the air when you professed to all you knew that God isn't real, and if He is, who really cares?" So you see, turn your will to God, and He'll keep you from that big mistake. Don't listen to the fools whose life was cruel, filling your head and telling you lies, that God and Jesus are fake.

CHRISTMAS WISH

Christmas is the time of year, where all fears should be put aside, as we sing with joyful cheers, oh how they ring with pride.

Not all children get to feel this bliss, but in their hearts, they should sing in times like this.

Why does it take Christmas to soften our smiles? We go all year long, changing our moods like a lost and lonely child.

We're constantly looking for the right color of the day, that will soothe our hearts and melt the darkness and pave our way.

Christmas is filled with many colors that we seek, it lifts our spirit and changes those who long to be meek.

The smells of Christmas overwhelm our minds; the candles, the cookies, the scent of trees, the white winter chill, filled with a clean winter's breeze.

When the eve is over and the children are at rest, we should give God praise, for He is the very best.

The morning comes and the children are alive, they go through their presents with a blinding drive.

The eggnog is consumed as the presents are strewn, from one end to the other, in this joyful room.

God looks down from the sky and shows His love, through the hearts of many who keep their eyes to the heavens above.

After the clutter and clatter is done, the parents and their little ones should praise the Lord, then the children can play and have their fun. This day has brought many friends together, and all ill thoughts have been put to rest; now the night is nearly over, and the day must end, and the friends must leave for their homes and return to their old ways again.

DO NOT COMPLAIN

Think not of what you don't have, but what you might gain. If you're willing to accept the terms of your life and refrain from bitterness at what can't be changed.

Look at life as a process, a school inside your head; to become one of God's successes, opening your heart to His undying love, living in the spirit, so you may be led.

For what you see in others can become an asset and help you reform those old thoughts you had; to transform in His glorious sight, using the strength God has given you, be it daytime or night.

Remember, do not complain, for if your life becomes stained at times, just remember this simple little rhyme…

Think of all the crippled children of the world who seem like they've got it bad; in their hearts and in their minds, God gives them the strength for what lies ahead in time.

From Madness to Jesus

THE ROSE

How sweet the rose, the scent forgiving,
Its beauty unsurpassed, with petals of velvet,
with definitions enchanting.
Their colors so brilliant, with vibrancy and vigor,
Fills one's heart to capacity, calling on feelings untold.
To share but one rose with someone is more hope
than understanding during difficult moments,
it represents love and compassion for two, but to
those who feel nothing, it has none.

ONE OF ONE

Two people can live as one, as long as there is embracing love; their strength can increase and numbers will build, when their souls are joined with God and Jesus in the heavens above.

No one can unfold the many layers that have been bonded through many fears and untold prayers.

Fear can be a weapon, a destruction for both sides, but joined together, they can go through life without having to run and hide.

They can beat and overcome any obstacle and survive, as long as they remain with God as one, they can still feel like they're alive.

For death is easy and living is hard, it can be very simple if you're willing to try real hard.

There's no guarantee if you can't see through the haze, that uncertainty and fear, that eternal blaze.

Darkness will always pass by, waiting anxiously forever, for you to blink your eyes.

Standing side by side is sometimes not enough, but holding hands and gripping tight, these bonds a love that is so strong, that as one with God, you can't go wrong.

Dreams are meant to be shared, through thoughts and trust by two who care.

Alone and unfeeling are two vicious words, that no one should feel or even be heard.

They can rip at your heart, so you won't be able to feel, you will continue to feel pain, and they will make you unreal. I'm tired of battling for what may seem right, all along knowing its fear in me that wants to fight.

I now join my hands and through God, bond with my heart, to become open and feeling and ask God to help the old ways depart.

With God by my side, I will go through thick and thin, because in the end, I know I'll win.

God knows I try, and now I'll begin, to know what it's like to be my own best friend.

Can you relate so far... but wait, there's more!

NO REGRETS

Being taught is a process that can't be denied, I say I know, I know, but it has all been a lie.

I've said things I've done, I've done things I've said,

But if I don't give them to Jesus, the words won't rest in my head.

They say reality is a concept and the truth really hurts, but it's time to take back the key and quit holding onto my mother's skirt.

The fears we feel can be a defect in our lives, but I feel it can be changed to better our quest for life.

Behold the real me inside, the one who holds onto inadequacy and false pride.

I am a man who really wants to change, I can no longer wear the mask, running around this world acting bitter and strange.

I don't need the things of this world, you see, all I need is God, Christ Jesus, and their love. This I know I will receive.

So see me now, and don't forget, that I am who I am by the grace of God and I wish to live my life with no regrets.

God's Strength

Standing alone with the wind in my face, I look to the sky with feelings of disgrace.

Once again, I ask God for His forgiveness of my sinful past, praying for my pain as I ask, "God, how long will this last?"

Then I feel His presence and His open arms; I feel life in me, I can feel it stir, my mind searching for answers and situations to occur.

I've looked in my past and seen what I've done, not going anywhere or even having any fun.

I've tried and I've tried to make ends meet, but the outcome was always the same, so I would accept defeat.

But when I have God's book in my hands and His love in my heart, I can feel a new beginning, as I get a fresh start.

There's one thing I've learned and that's how to be real, to let God search my soul and now He shows me how to feel.

There were many desperate attempts at life's rolling hills, now God has given me new strength without any chills.

I need to be reborn, to walk through the pain; with a new meaning to life, there's nothing I can't gain.

I have two good hands to do God's work, by placing them together and praying for someone else, I can show others of His miracles and gain love for myself.

777

The year of the Lord is upon us, and our thoughts should be feelings of love. Set your sights on His wonderful miracles, like the flight of the snow-white dove.

We will be judged one day and stand in front of His mighty throne, for our sins before us will ultimately be shown.

Don't try to be perfect, just do your best, because Jesus is watching while judging all the rest.

Satan had his year in 666 and nothing was shown, for if evil had run rampant, many who didn't believe surely would have known.

Look at the signs and listen to the new prophets expound words from the Lord, but be careful, test the spirits, because Satan is deceitful and behind the curtain the lion will roar.

I can't wait until the Rapture comes to pass, as non-believers will blame it on aliens or, Hmm, it must have been that mysterious swamp gas.

God is still there, and Jesus at His side, don't give up by taking the mark, or it will be your demise.

So etch in your mind the numbers of the Lord, instill peace in your heart, for evil soon will come when the Holy Spirit must depart.

TIMES HEALS ALL

It's time you see, to heal the child in me, to break these bonding chains; it's a life gone past in a steadfast way, not allowing ourselves the pleasures of life to flow free.

I've seen no future in my growing years, but I have seen myself in loneliness, shedding many, many tears.

Bouncing around from place to place, hiding my head in shame; the games I've played and the people I've hurt, I ran from the truth when I should have stayed.

But now that I've seen the life I've led, it's very apparent to see, it's time to change and free the guilt, this shame inside of me.

God helped me change to become the real me; He lifts the fog telling me this, "My son, I can give you so much more, just ask, My gifts are free and they're yours."

Time is nothing where my life is concerned, I place my soul in your hands, my heart is filled with love Lord God, so see me now as I wave my hands high in the stands.

So God, You helped me remember my innocent ways, and with Your strength, I'll show You I can endure and return from a life of shameful dismay.

CHASING THE BREEZE

The curtains are drawn as we watch the sky emit darker shades, bringing on destined thoughts of a storm the clouds have made.

As a child, we dream of being anyone we want without any torments and wasted taunts.

We see the breeze begin to blow, and the outcome is evident; this we know.

The swaying trees and the swings that do their dance, we think things over, that we might take a chance.

Always wanting to chase the breeze, trying to catch the things the wind has seized.

This is life chasing the dream, frantically searching for endless schemes while trying to balance on a shaky narrow beam.

In this vast world, there is only one true dream, for God is the only one who can silence our lonely screams.

He teaches us to extend our hands while asking for His gracious gifts; then He'll warm our hearts and cleanse our minds if we slow our pace and just give Him time.

GROWING

Warm air flows like beams of light, and there are few that see the purpose of flight.

Flapping their wings, as if tied to strings, the beauty of their grace is the mystery of things,

Observing them float on that stream of air, we often think, this just isn't fair.

Looking down the narrow path, we see much more than whispering grass.

Their carefree flight is so loose with life that we imagine, what if we could touch someone with what they do to our sight.

More often than not, we forget when we leave, the things we've seen that made us weave.

Their moves are an elixir in itself, but some would prefer to see them in a case upon their shelf.

Beauty is something to be observed, to savor for the time when someone has struck a nerve.

Life can be tough at times, you see, so remember the butterfly and how they grow to learn the gift of flight from the trees.

PAIN

It feels so real at times; we think of things and we think of rhymes.

It's so thoughtless and true that pain is a crime when you feel it, hurts you.

Some people have no guilt or remorse; they can only think of themselves of course.

So when someone hurts your heart and you feel there's no way you can forgive, just turn to Jesus, and He'll remove that thorn, so you can move forward and live.

Remember that pain is real, but God says you don't have to cry. Because of Him He can remove the pain, and to pain you can say goodbye.

TRUTH

God teaches us to confess our sins and put our lies behind.

It's time to see the truth and abide by His rules, and ask God for His love and His special tools.

To talk to Him not just in our times of need, I ask Him for everything, even the smallest thing; like the tiny mustard seed.

We think we're fooling God when we continue to use those little lies, but God has many angels, and He uses them for spies.

They build and build, those little white lies; they poison our spirit and become our demise.

The more we practice the honest ways, the more we gain, and it shows in our displays.

It's a new life that we bring to you, a feeling of God's holy bliss, showing you life in another way, accepting Jesus and His loving kiss.

I Can't Explain

I can't explain to those who complain how life is meant to be, but I can explain to those who are willing to see how God wants us to act and the gifts He has for you and me.

In the book of Romans, it tells us how to live with others according to God's word, to live without fear of what we can't explain while trying to figure out what we've heard.

Because when we're not in the light of the Lord, we try to rationalize our lives, though tragically lashing out with a double-edged sword.

Leading a double life of good and bad will keep us confused, angry, and mad.

This comes from the torment inside, an unwillingness to let God take away those unnerving thoughts of fear and unexplainable pride.

I speak of fear and pride all too often because it was a blanket that Satan waved before my eyes, a red flag of hate that covered my feelings, and to all I felt despise.

Fear and pride are spelled two different ways; I can't explain it, you have to decipher and learn for yourself what they portray.

For fear is pride and pride is fear, one is weakness, and the other is unwilling to hear.

So if we're unable to drop our pride, we can't humble ourselves before God, so into fear we run and hide.

Just remember, God will remove all our fears and help us learn what we can't explain, for He knows all truth and all we've ever felt, including our suffering and pain.

IRRITABLE TWINGE

When everything seems to be going so good, you suddenly feel the presence of evil, now go to your knees and do what you should.

This is a time to get with the Lord, to increase your faith, not become lazy and bored.

That irritable twinge being the evil one, he can feel any gaps in your soul; they can supply the evil that is on your back, and soon you're caught and under attack.

Satan is so quick to pierce our hearts and make our tempers short, that our minds become blank and unable to sort.

By the blood of Jesus, we can rebuke this demon and send him on his way, because we no longer desire its presence and no longer want him to stay.

The power of Christ is our strongest defense; without Him in our lives, nothing would really make any sense.

I know this to be true because it's working as I speak, that Satan's evil demon has lost its grip and become weak.

It's the power of Christ that makes all evil cringe, the mighty lightning bolt from heaven, and to them, their spirit does singe.

I've learned a valuable lesson today, that no matter how often you pray, Satan is patiently waiting for your anger to stir and your mind to go astray.

LOW HANGING BOARD

Through darkness we scurry like hungry little rats, searching for anything, even a tit-for-tat.

An endless dream and scores of dead ends, a loss of many and many dead friends.

The nights were cold, the days were long, but nothing could hurt us because in our minds, we were bold and strong.

It was a false belief, a dream of our own, our darkened hearts would be all alone.

Nothing could stand in our way because we were the ones that would rule the day!

So we thought to ourselves at the end of the line, where do I go now, there's no more time.

We've run out of rope, and we're hanging by a thread. We bow our heads in shame and wish we were dead.

We're weak and frail like a child, our heads are spinning, and our minds are running wild.

Frantic thoughts clog our minds; where do I go? I'm so afraid, I just don't know!

With tears filling our eyes, and we're bound on our knees, we admit defeat and ask God to help us with our disease.

He smiles and is pleased when He sees a sinner bow before Him, praying on their knees.

God reaches inside and heals your heart, He renews your mind and gives you a fresh start.

So if you choose not to believe in the ways of the Lord, just keep running in darkness, and you'll soon run into that low-hanging board!

THE ETERNAL QUEST FOR CHRIST

My newfound journey on my quest for Christ has made me learn that there's so much more to life.

It's more than just being alive; it's like dying and being reborn again, except now I have love and a true friendship that will never end.

I can go anywhere, no matter what kind of day it may be, and I know for a fact that God and Jesus will always be there for me.

It's a relief to know there will always be someone who cares, even though I may be alone, and there's no one there.

Each day I feel the peace I gain as the darkness fades, feelings of belonging that my God has made.

I've stumbled and fell like a newborn babe; I now rejoice at the choice I made, and this time I decided to stay.

The walk is not that hard if you listen to the words, the inner peace you will find in His book you just heard.

God's book will take you wherever your mind wants to go, to the gates of heaven or down to Satan's hellish hole.

Because it talks of men who have given their lives to Christ and those who defied God and lost their lives.

The choice is all up to you, what you make of it will be your gift to God. That's all He wants, for you to quit wallowing in the worldly sod.

I feel God's purpose; He wants to hold our souls in His loving arms and to feel He's saved us from Satan and his devilish charms.

KNOW YOUR ENEMY

There once was a young man who was taught the ways of the Lord, and he followed his path, blazing a trail with his mighty sword.

His walk was strong, and his heart was clean, so he continued daily for his Father to be seen.

He saw new sights as he started each day, through endless barriers, his strength never gave way.

This youth depended on God's daily word that filled his spirit as he marveled at the passing birds.

His journey seemed so easy as he trusted the Lord, but soon it was so simple, and his mind became bored.

One day he felt so strong, he veered from his path; he felt invincible from any unjustly wrath.

In his mind, he thought he was able to stray; his mind did wander, and he felt there was no need to pray.

Well, on his journey, everything went too smooth; he thought to himself, "I can do anything, there's no way I can lose."

Suddenly, he came upon a path that led up towards the sky; its trail was smooth and wide and wound endlessly way up high.

Feeling there wasn't anything he couldn't conquer on his own, he started up the path and found he was not alone.

He heard a rattle that made him jump with fear; it was a rattlesnake, and these words he did hear!

"Oh, young one, could you help an old rattlesnake that doesn't have the strength to climb? Your help would be appreciated; you would save me so much time." The boy stood back from the snake with his sword held high and said, "Why should I help you up the path towards the sky? You'll just bite me, and I'll live no more and die."

From Madness to Jesus

The snake said, "I promise you, I will not attack; all I want is a lift inside your sack."

The boy felt his independent courage return as he helped the rattlesnake and forgot all that he had learned.

Well, the day was hot, and the trail was long; he felt so strong that nothing could go wrong.

As he reached the peak, he let out a great cheer, "I made it to the top!" Suddenly, the rattlesnake he did hear!

"Let me out, and I'll be on my way, and we'll end this journey on this long hot day."

The boy reached into his sack and laid the snake on the ground; he went to stand up, feeling pain as he fell upon the ground.

"You bit me!" the young boy cried, "You promised me it wouldn't be so!"

The snake replied, "Oh yes, indeed I did, but you knew who I was, and you should have known."

The moral of the story is, oh yes, we should beware that Satan is waiting for us with his tricky evil snares.

This comes when we think we've learned it all; but guess what? God tells us to beware, test the spirits, and don't rely on your own judgment, for when we do, we can easily be led astray, and Satan will use us in a role for his sickly little play.

I hope the poems God and I have shared with you can help you overcome those fears that we hide and those differences you have experienced in life, trying to figure out what to do. I thought that by sharing my life and what I have learned through treatment, life, the acceptance of Jesus Christ, and showing you God's true love, I might help others such as myself gain insight, that we are not alone anymore!

Putting my trials and errors on paper might help you process the troubles that we face daily, past and present, so that we might get a better perspective instead of someone pointing the finger telling us that "this is your problem, and this is what you need to do about it."

Sometimes it's hard to accept we have a problem, let alone have someone point out our faults. I would like to leave you with two last thoughts to ponder that may or may not help you to remember: that if there is no change, there is no change! This first one I try to read daily, but not always.

It has helped me look back at what I need to do if I want godly time in my life and to live life the way God wants me to.

I Am My Final Authority

With God, I am my final authority for everything that I do. This means I accept full responsibility for the consequences of my actions.

When someone confronts me on my behavior, I need to tell myself, I benefit from my mistakes and I don't need to belittle myself when I make them. It only causes grief for myself and others around me. I have to get out of my past and stay in the here and now. I won't blame others for my problems, mistakes, and defeats of my past. I have to realize that my life before can no longer continue to affect my recovery.

As a well-known writer once said, "My life has been soul murder, shame-based." I am shame, but through God, I don't have to accept it. I have to purge myself of any shame, blame, guilt, or remorse of my past if I want quality time in my life. I've been a loner when it came to help from others because I was in control; was I really? Now I need to seek support no matter how bad my ego hurts. All the time I spent in treatment, every counselor told me I needed to learn how to be humble. Humble to me was humiliation, a word I couldn't comprehend. I would have never in my wildest dreams thought I could learn to be humble from a woman, but I did. Being humble was the hardest thing to learn in my whole life, but when I did, my pride followed, and then I found my way back to God and accepted Jesus Christ as my personal savior.

The way my life was before, I always liked a challenge, the tougher, the better. Now I have to accept every problem and goal as a challenge to my recovery and my awareness. I've based life around approval from others, but never complimented them for telling me so. I always accepted them and stuffed them into my egotistical mind. From now on, I will not always depend on others for approval just to feed my egotistical child. My child always expects everyone to take the initiative to approach me for personal contact; this has got to change.

I have to take the initiative; otherwise, I think people are avoiding me. When I've thought this, I'm sure others get the message, "the walls are up, there's no use talking to him." Throughout my life, I've slowly but surely taken happiness I saw going on around me and mistook it for a liability, something I could discard easily. I've been so miserable all these years that I couldn't believe anybody could have happiness in their lives.

I've been so wrapped up in the pain from the past that I couldn't see any hope or happiness for my future. I've never feared any man, but I have feared what man has to say, especially the truth.

Now there is only one I fear, and that one is God. May you find Him now! I've accepted put downs and insults all my life; I just stuffed them or laughed them off. From now on, I will not accept any condemnations, put downs, or insults because they will destroy my recovery and my relationship with God. I shall face reality and resist, nothing I cannot change.

God is good, and He is good all the time.

I would like all of us to remember that God doesn't push the erase button, but through His Son and true repentance, He throws away all our sins into the sea of forgetfulness.

He does not erase all our debts, nor the harm we have inflicted upon others. What He does do in time is change our hearts and renew your mind through His Word. Thus, others will see who we have become through God's grace and mercy.

We would all like to think that it is just because we accepted Jesus that everyone should immediately forgive us for our past. We must remember all the times we said we would change; and after time, we often revert to our old ways again just because someone pissed us off, or the dog died or just because I deserved it, really? They have heard our stories and our true desire to change, but until they see a long-term determination and feel that they can trust us again, we have to be patient. I know it's hard, but time heals all, and in God's time, not ours.

WHY WE RUN IN FEAR?

We see the candle; its flame dancing with every sudden movement. It emits a soothing aura surrounded by soft edges. If we were to reach for the flame and try to extinguish it, the flame would reject our touch and show us pain, in turn making us recoil in fear.

Fear that makes us hide from the jaws of life that seem to be endlessly nipping at our heels. This is our nature, not God's. Letting God take our pain gives us the courage to extinguish the flame without rejection, because, though it may hurt, we know who to turn to if the pain becomes too much. This is life, and there is a God. You know the amusing thing about most people? They would rather run and hide instead of facing our fears and suffer the way Jesus did. Hey, the pain only hurts until it goes away. But we would rather run, taking the candle with us wherever we may go, so we alone can strike that match, igniting the flame over and over again, so we can feel our hands reject that soft soothing light.

The end

Praise the Lord and His Son Jesus Christ!

1. Thank you God for always being there for me.
2. Thank you God for the insight ability you gave me.
3. Thank you God for putting a roof over my head, and food in my stomach.
4. Thank you God for putting the people in my life who really care.
5. Thank you God for always protecting me from harm.
6. Thank you God for the gifts of life I've received.
7. Thank you God for helping me walk through my resentments.
8. Thank you God for your miracles that show me your power and your strength and wisdom to share them with others.
9. Thank you God for a life worth saving…
10. Thank you God for showing me how many times I've promised to you and never kept them, but now you've shown me your true power.

~THANK YOU GOD!~

www.ingramcontent.com/pod-product-compliance
Lightning Source LLC
LaVergne TN
LVHW051543070426
835507LV00021B/2380